HIRSCHFELD'S WORLD

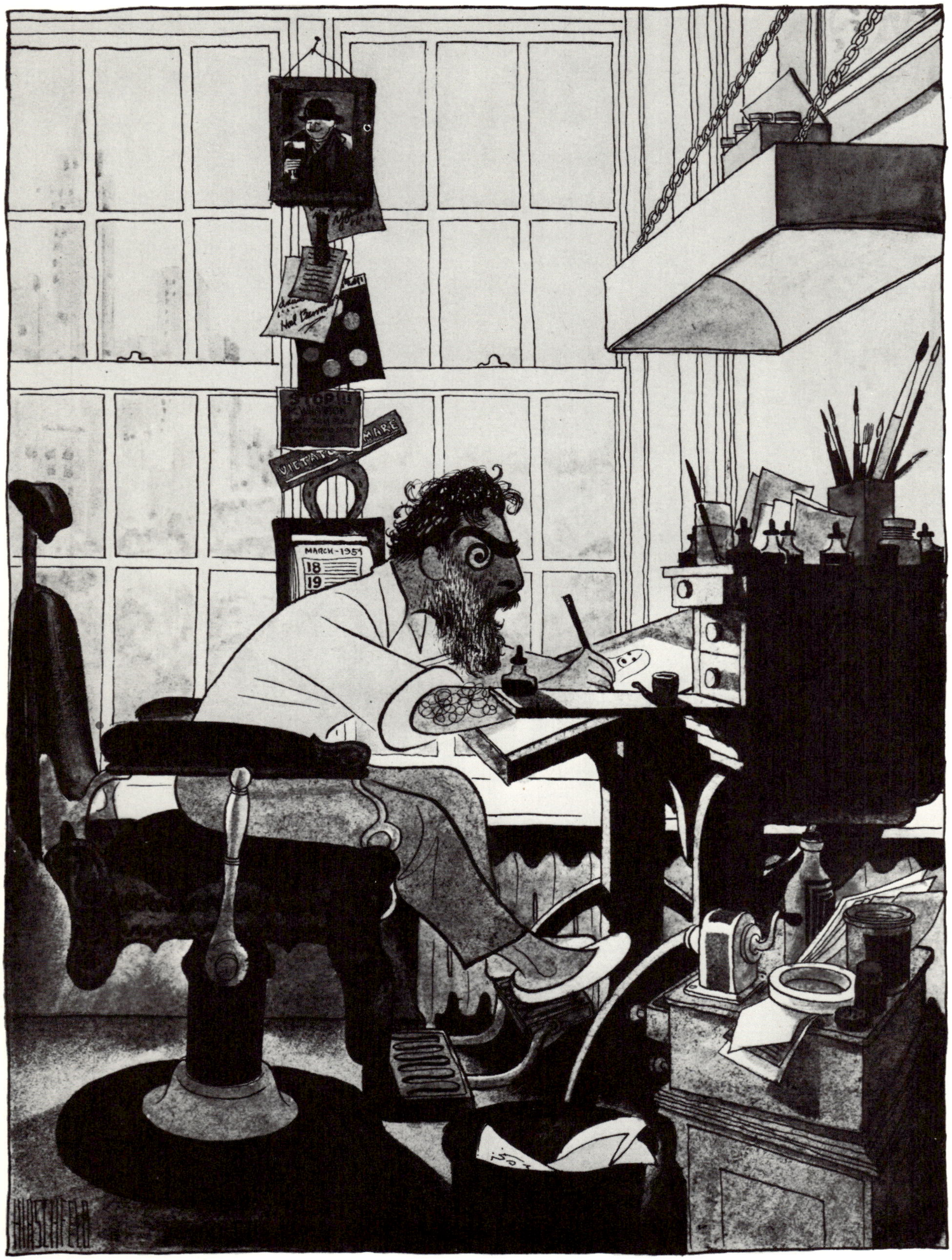
STOP!!!
VIETATO
MARE
MARCH-1959
18
19
HIRSCHFELD

HIRSCHFELD'S WORLD

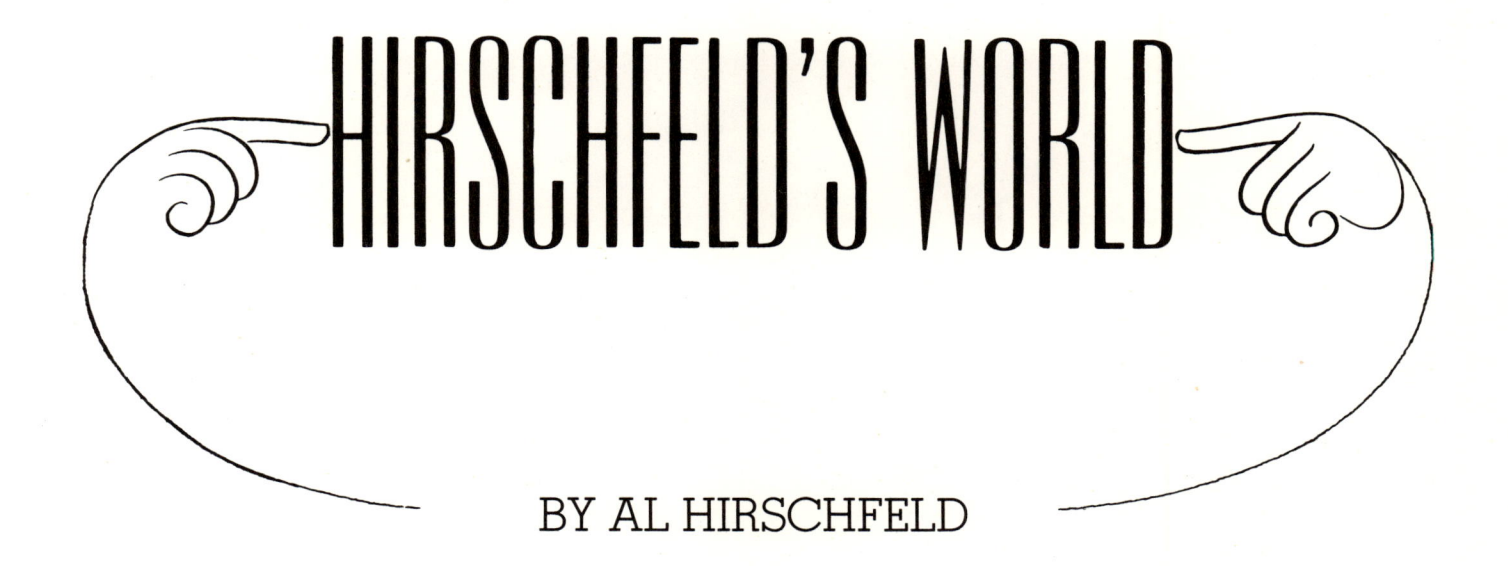

BY AL HIRSCHFELD

Introduction by Lloyd Goodrich
Director Emeritus, Whitney Museum of American Art, New York

Harry N. Abrams, Inc., Publishers, New York

To Dolly, without whose help this book and Nina would never have been conceived.

Frontispiece: "Self-portrait in my barber chair, in my old studio on top of the Osborne at Fifty-seventh Street and Seventh Avenue." 1940s

Compiled and edited by Marti Malovany and Sheila Franklin

Designed by Dirk Luykx

Library of Congress Cataloging in Publication Data
Hirschfeld, Albert.
  Hirschfeld's world.
  Edition published in 1970 under title: The world of Hirschfeld.
  Includes index.
  1. Theater—Caricatures and cartoons. 2. Moving-pictures—Caricatures and cartoons. 3. American wit and humor, Pictorial. I. Title. II. Title: World.
NC1429. H527A4 1981   741.5'973   80-26621
ISBN 0-8109-2245-2 (pbk.)

© 1981 Albert Hirschfeld

Published in 1981 by Harry N. Abrams, Incorporated, New York
All rights reserved. No part of the contents of this book may be reproduced without the written permission of the publishers

Printed and bound in the United States of America

CONTENTS

Introduction by Lloyd Goodrich   7

HIRSCHFELD'S WORLD by Al Hirschfeld   11

Early Lithographs   37

Theater   43

Movies   77

Personalities   117

Portrait of the Artist   153

Index   159

Acknowledgments   160

INTRODUCTION

Caricature is usually considered a negative art. The word suggests hostility and malice. It implies distortion of truth. Artistically it is regarded as narrow concentration on the victim's physiognomy, and of only minor aesthetic importance.

Al Hirschfeld's art triumphantly refutes all these misconceptions. There is nothing negative about it; its humor, while sharp-edged, is affirmative and gay. It takes all kinds of liberties with literal facts, but it grasps essential truth of character. And as art, Hirschfeld's drawings are the work of a highly sophisticated artist who uses the graphic medium to create rich and vital design.

Hirschfeld began as a student of painting, drawing, and sculpture, and it was on a foundation of thorough schooling and experience as an artist that his graphic style was built. He spent most of the 1920's in Paris, painting and making prints, and his lithographs from those years reveal a skillful draftsman fully aware of what was going on in the international art scene. Then in the mid-1920's—almost by accident, as he tells it—he began drawing for newspapers; from then on his weekly contributions, particularly in *The New York Times*, have delighted millions of fans all over the country.

One of the obvious but basic facts about Hirschfeld is that he can draw—an accomplishment that is not as common as one might suppose. No matter how far his drawings may depart from literalism, they are always based on understanding of the forms and movements of the human body, and on sure skill in putting them down on paper.

The caricaturist and the portrait painter, though they may seem to inhabit different artistic worlds, are not too far removed. The masters of portraiture have never confined themselves to the sitter's external appearance; they have aimed for fundamental character, and in the process have taken considerable liberties with surface facts. The caricaturist does the same; but with him, happily, liberty becomes license.

Hirschfeld's caricatures, like the work of the portraitist, are founded on an unerring sense of character—a rare gift, and one that must be inborn and cannot be learned in schools. The individual's face, body, hands, clothes, gestures, attitudes, facial expressions, and all the things that make him a human being unlike anybody else in the world—these traits are isolated, distilled, and concentrated into a pictorial image that embodies his essential uniqueness, purified of the dull norm.

But here the caricaturist parts company with the portraitist. Taking an individual's characteristics, Hirschfeld plays on them with maximum freedom and inventiveness, magnifies salient traits, distorts scale and proportion, and produces an image that is both fantasy and essential truth. His portraits need no identifying labels; they are more like the person than the person himself. The immediate recognition we get from them is due not to any laborious assembling of details but to the artist's instantaneous grasp of the total personality. His caricature is no mere mechanical enlargement of faces and features, but a creative play with basic forms.

Hirschfeld's favorite field, the theater, has given him rich opportunities to exercise these gifts. In the theater a central element is the portrayal of character, and his pictorial portrayals of the actors' living portrayals are character double-distilled. At the same time, his players are seen with an ever-present humor that is not malicious, that laughs with the comedian, mocks the overserious, and exposes pomposity and phoniness for what they are.

The theater is also an art of physical action, from the studied gestures and attitudes of the straight performers to the acrobatics of dancers; and here again the theater offers inexhaustible material for Hirschfeld's highly developed sense of movement. Every figure in his drawings is in motion, slow or swift, stately or wild. His dancers defy the law of gravity. In his musical comedy scenes we can hear the music.

This mastery of movement is not just the picturing of figures in action, but the embodying of movement itself; his drawings are dynamic creations in moving line and form. The line is alive; it leaps, races around curves, zooms with whiplash speed. Every line has rhythm and plays its precise part in an overall linear ballet.

His line is highly varied. It ranges from thick to thin, from bold, sweeping outlines to the fine, delicate lines of interior forms and distant figures and objects. Foreground and background are created not only by differences in scale but by contrasted heaviness or lightness of line. It is a virtuoso line; it can carve a face, simulate hair and whiskers, describe a dancer's leap, caress a chorus girl's thighs.

Hirschfeld realizes that the physical language of graphic art is two-dimensional—in his case, black ink on white illustrator's board—and that the artist should respect this flatness and build his art on it, while exploiting these seemingly limited resources to the full. His pictures always speak to the eye in direct physical terms. All his black-and-white drawings are in flat black; only rarely does he use tone. Looking at them one is apt to forget that they are to be reproduced by the simplest printing method, linecut, without use of the photoengraver's screen. There are never any shadows or any attempt at photographic representation. Sometimes forms are modeled in line, but most often they are drawn in outline. He has an uncanny ability to suggest roundness with pure outlines. Actualities are translated into graphic images; eyes become circles, slits, spirals. Zero Mostel's unshaven chin is a checkerboard of lines and dots.

What fun he has with clothes! The theater offers an infinite variety of costumes, of every period and fashion, every degree of elaborateness or near-nudity. An eighteenth-century hat, with its flamboyant piling up of feathers and flowers and ribbons, produces a fantastic pictorial image that is both funny and at the same time enchanting as pure pattern.

The theater is also an art of spectacle, of planned settings and ensembles, of visual as well as verbal drama. Hirschfeld makes the most of these spectacular aspects. His compositions are often extremely complex, with all kinds of happenings going on simultaneously. The ridiculousness of much of this expensive pageantry does not escape his humorous eye. But his compositions are faithful to the theatrical law of giving the center of the stage to the leading players, and of making the whole elaborate production culminate in the stars. In this and other respects, his drawings are in themselves great theater.

To me one of the continuing mysteries is how, out of this enormous treasure house of imagery, Hirschfeld succeeds in producing, once a week or oftener, designs of such complexity, completeness, and control. The relations of line to line, the contrast of dynamic forms and empty space, the balance of blacks and whites, the rhythmic interplay of every element—all are built up into designs that are strong, unified, and right. This achievement can be due only to a gifted creative artist expressing himself naturally about a world that he knows in every detail, and loves.

    In a day when humorous illustration, by and large, has declined to the level of the weakly drawn illustrated joke, Hirschfeld is one of the few masters of graphic humor. With no need for gag lines, his drawings speak for themselves, in the potent language of pure graphic art.

Lloyd Goodrich
Director Emeritus, Whitney Museum of
American Art, New York

HIRSCHFELD'S WORLD

When I am confronted seriously with the unanswerable question, "What is a caricature?" or "How do you manage to capture a likeness?" I pin my questioner with a profound stare and blubber reasonable nonsense. The arbitrary mantle of "authority" with which I endow myself allows me to function as a social creature. But the answers are satisfying solely as conversation—when I am alone, staring at a blank piece of illustration board, trying to render a likeness or caricature, I really do not have a clue to help me. I am not at all sure whether or not my drawings even *are* "caricatures." I would feel more comfortable being classified as a "characterist," if there were such a word or school. All I know for certain is that the "capturing of a likeness" is of secondary importance to me and serves merely as stimulant or catalyst—a sort of springboard for an unpredictable dive into the unknown. My primary interest is in producing a drawing capable of surviving the obvious fun of recognition or news value. The drawing—or lack of it—is all that matters.

Fortunately, I have never been at a loss for subject matter, for the subject which turns me on is people. No matter where I go, anywhere in the world, there they are: stimulating, challenging people. I frankly admit my limitations as a photographic recorder of Nature. I am not against it, but there is nothing I can do with it. I find Nature a great place to visit, but I would not care to live there. The adventure and mystery of a smoke-filled room disappear with fresh air and sunlight. As an example, it would never occur to me to sit on the lip of the Grand Canyon and copy it in paint on a small piece of canvas. I consider the Grand Canyon already painted and as pure subject matter it holds no more interest for me than a

1 Prince of Wales. 1937

decayed molar dramatically lit. The only difference from a visual point of view is that the Grand Canyon is bigger.

I suppose that anatomical exaggeration, as Funk and Wagnalls point out, is essential in caricature, but I have never subscribed to the notion that this form of primitive humor is either witty or, with its limited objective, one of man's nobler achievements. Caricatures based solely on physical distortion have the mutual ugliness of an academic eye, ear, nose, and throat portrait. A photograph of an actor reflected in a Coney Island distortion mirror or seen through an empty jelly jar may capture a distorted "likeness" of the actor, but its true reflection, from my point of view, is a critical assessment of the photographer. I do not like caricatures of big heads and little bodies, nor do I care for distorted photo caricatures; and it is distressing to realize that millions of readers and most editors do not agree with me that the arbitrary shrinking or enlarging of human organs is no funnier than a medical drawing of a ruptured appendix.

All drawings in pure line are to some degree abstract. The magic of "drawn symbols" or "written words" is interrelated and requires similar intelligence to understand. The problem I have created for myself is to translate a specific person or object in legible symbols so that the reader, when confronted with my arrangement of lines, will recognize their meaning as clearly as he would the letter *A*. When this alchemy takes place, the likeness is automatic. To illustrate further: Why, in common experience, do we recognize a friend approaching from a great distance? He may be wearing a new hat and coat, his features covered with a muffler, but details such as these are of no importance in establishing recognition. The approaching figure is the friend and there is no question about it. The magic of this built-in radar, which does not depend on the seeing of features or the recognition of clothes for identification, is the sort of mystery I have spent a lifetime trying to unravel.

The enigma of personality is elusive. The adventure of translating personality into graphic symbols defies classification. Even when it is fully realized it does not explain itself. I consider a successful likeness has been achieved when the subject begins to look like the drawing rather than the other way around. A successful likeness communicates itself immediately, unquestionably, magically, and unreasonably. The problem of creating this caricature without really understanding how it is done is the common frustration of most serious caricaturists and without doubt accounts for the fact that so many of them retire by garroting—and other self-destructive antisocial means.

The unquestioned acceptance of publicized "images" may make life easier for the cartoonist and reader but the problem for the caricaturist becomes compounded. The banal use, over and over again, of plagiarized symbols brainwashes the cartoonist and reader into uncritical judgment of likeness or of the character of the personality depicted. The distinction I make between "cartoon" and "caricature" is arbitrary and purely personal. In my vocabulary they have become critical estimates, rather than descriptive words distinguishing two distinct art forms. The use, in cartoons, of identifying labels, clearly spelled out, appended to an ineptly drawn subject, is a toe-curling admission of honest incompetence. An unsolved drawing of a woman knitting a sweater is not enhanced as a drawing by labeling the woman "Israel" and the sweater "the spirit of Jewish consciousness."

Animated cartoons started out as pure caricature. A line appeared on the cinema screen and it drew itself into a figure whose belly button danced in wild abandon; a gnome played a flute and the musical notes pouring out of the instrument were used as a ladder for him to climb into eternity. The art was pure; audiences accepted the form with enthusiasm. The corruption was slow, insidious, and bit by bit the literalness of the story took over and the drawings were used to club the spectator into submission. Communication in caricature must tell its story in abstract line. The limitation of the medium is an integral part of its message—the purity of line, apart from the likeness, is its own message. Marshall McLuhan's succinct philosophy "the medium is the message" is an apt description of caricature. On the other hand, "a word is worth a thousand pictures" is an apt description of cartooning.

In 1924 I moved to Paris, settling on its Left Bank, to become a painter. Before that, apart from an occasional drawing for publication, my ambition was to be a sculptor. I lost interest in both sculpture and painting as I matured. One day I may recapture my romance with these forms, but for the past fifty-some-odd years I have never had reason to doubt my enduring love of line. In Paris, during those halcyon years, I grew a beard, wore wooden sabots, corduroy pants, lumberjack shirts, and seriously painted in oil on Belgian canvas. Most of my paintings were really drawings in color, and my drawings were really sketches for paintings. Neither had form or made much sense—both forms suffered from a lack of talent. After much experimenting in varied media I found, at least for a brief period,

2   Martha Graham. 1938

3 Change-of-address card. 1927

watercolor more amenable to my gifts, but this infatuation never went beyond the flirtation stage. My real sense of satisfaction, then as now, was the image in pure line. More and more the line made undeniable demands on my time and energies. It is now no longer a matter of choice. The line seems to have developed a life of its own, my control over it being constantly challenged. One line juxtaposed against another causing anxiety, frustration, joy; the addition of a meaningful line causing happiness; the erasure of an extraneous one; the making of self-made problems to be solved by self-made solutions—these are the things that have paid my rent and allowed me to live like any other prosperous capitalist.

In 1931 I was still toying with the unrewarding chore of copying Nature—in oil and watercolor—and establishing myself as a serious painter. Exhibitions in Paris, St. Louis, New York, and Chicago were received with great kindness by the art critics. A watercolor was accepted by the St. Louis Museum of Art for its permanent collection. But all this ended that same year when I first set foot on the island of Bali in the Dutch East Indies, which are now Indonesia.

The Balinese sun seemed to bleach out all color, leaving everything in pure line. The people became line drawings walking around. I think it no accident that rich, lush painting flourishes in the fog of Europe, while graphic art—from Egypt across Persia to India and all the way to the Pacific Islands—is influenced by the sun. At any rate it was in Bali that my attraction to drawing blossomed into an enduring love affair with line. I am much more influenced by the drawings of Harunobu, Utamaro, and Hokusai than I am by the painters of the West. Mass media communications may subtly be changing East and West cultures, and the day may arrive when the whole world becomes one great big integrated garage. In the meantime I prefer the vast differences.

At that time I was the only American resident on Bali, and, quite naturally, lured an occasional guest from the round-the-world steamship cruises that stopped at the island regularly. One day, two fellows arrived and introduced themselves—Sidney and Charlie Chaplin. Before the day was over we became fast friends. They abandoned ship and checked into the recently constructed and sole hotel in south Bali. The motion picture was unknown in Bali, and on discovering his anonymity Charlie decided to carry out an experiment. It was then I realized that the mustache, baggy pants, and oversized shoes were of no more importance to Chaplin than the type of quill used by Shakespeare or the frame on a Picasso.

A Man With Both Feet in the Clouds

4 Charlie Chaplin. 1942

His audience comprised seven houseboys who worked for me. Only one of these was actually in my employ. The rest were hired in turn, as assistants, by each of the others. Charlie proceeded to put the pith helmet that he carried with him on his head and it sprang crazily into the air, seemingly with a will of its own. Undaunted, and with a wide-eyed look of nonchalance, he tried it again. And again the hat flew off his head. The natives howled with laughter, thinking his hat possessed demoniac powers. When the simplicity of the trick was exposed to them they tried desperately, amid great hilarity, to snap their turbans in the air in the same way. That was the experiment: he had wanted to see if the Balinese would laugh at his pantomime. They did. This was his first day in Bali, and he had earned for himself the descriptive title of "funny man."

Years later I visited Charlie in Hollywood, and we talked of many things. He was in great form, dancing, laughing, and being the greatest pantomimist I had ever seen.

"Movement is liberated thought." He said this slowly, as though he had discovered a great truth. He stood up to clarify this point. "For instance, a spiral staircase goes this way," and he made a quick gesture with his hand and wrist. "Or a Balinese dancing girl is like this," and with the elegance of a ballet dancer he hopped about in staccato movement, his eyes wide and shifting back and forth like those of a spectator at a tennis match, his fingers nervously describing a delicate Chinese fan, his head imitating the detached, boneless, easy rhythm of a cobra. There she was, the little Balinese dancing girl, clear as a drawing.

I am frequently asked, "Are some people easier to caricature than others? Do you have any favorites?" The answer to that one is an easy "Yes, and I most certainly do." Of those still around I suppose Ray Bolger, Carol Channing, Jack Lemmon, Walter Matthau, Sammy Davis, Jr., Henry Fonda, Marlene Dietrich, Gwen Verdon, Bob Hope, and perhaps Jason Robards, Jr., look very much like my drawings of them. Years ago there were many more—Ed Wynn, Zero Mostel, Bert Lahr, Fred Allen, the Marx Brothers, Laurel and Hardy, Charlie Chaplin, any Barrymore, and Bing Crosby, to mention a few, but the actual listing would fill pages. All these public figures had one thing in common, apart from their insatiable appetite for the theater—they looked like their caricatures. The caricature, with its immediacy and almost trademark quality, became the image the public figure had been striving to become. Ray Bolger tells me that he has tried for years to imitate my drawings of

5 Zero Mostel in A FUNNY THING HAPPENED ON THE WAY TO THE FORUM. 1964

him. In actuality, I took the Ray Bolger he himself had invented, and (with an assist from God) reduced him to ink. His lack of respect for the rules of gravity, translated into line, became a dancing figure in space. Had it been Charlie Chaplin, for instance, the drawing would have looked entirely different, but the intent would have been the same.

   Years ago I was asked by a large agency in Pittsburgh to do six drawings of Garry Moore for a national publicity campaign. I had drawn Garry Moore on many previous occasions, which eliminated the necessity for time-consuming research. Within half an hour I finished what I thought to be an unmistakable likeness.

6 Ray Bolger in ALL AMERICAN. 1962

7 Carol Channing in HELLO, DOLLY! 1964

8   The "lucky" drawing of Garry Moore. 1967

Mildred Jones, who had been critic, housekeeper, and envy of all my friends for the past twenty-five years, passed my drawing table, saw the caricature, and in an unsolicited burst of enthusiasm guffawed, "Great! No doubt about it—that's him all right—I'd know him anywhere. Buster Keaton!" I knew then that I was in serious trouble. Rushing downstairs after this instant and enthusiastically positive false identification, I showed the drawing to my wife, demanding, "Who is it?" The lightning answer came without hesitation: "Buster Keaton." That was that. No question about it—but if this drawing was of Buster Keaton, then who the hell was Garry Moore and what did he look like?

    Days later—with literally thousands of sketches strewn across the studio floor, all looking like Buster Keaton—I decided to phone Pittsburgh and level with them. I no longer knew nor cared what Garry Moore looked like, I couldn't distinguish him from an orangutan. Whatever "wild talent" I possessed for caricature had disappeared, never to return. I would tell them, "God knows I have tried but I do not have the foggiest. Sorry, but those are the facts...." Mildred passed by my drawing table again, scanned the caricature of Buster Keaton and giggled, "Garry Moore—I've always liked him. Yessir—Garry Moore. What's he doin'? Coming back in a show?" Dashing downstairs with the drawing under my arm and bags under my eyes, I again confronted my wife. Holding the drawing aloft, and with just the slightest hysteria in my voice, I pleaded, "Who?" The instantaneous response: "Garry Moore."

Realizing the hopelessness of the situation, aware that the task of making five more—and different—drawings of Garry Moore was impossible for me to achieve, I conjured up the only solution possible. Grateful that Lady Luck made the one drawing possible, I photostatted that one and had six duplicates made. I pasted the photostatted heads on six different bodies representing the six different characters Mr. Moore was to portray. My wife, on seeing the finished product, assured me that if I sent these swindles to Pittsburgh they not only would refuse to pay for them, but in all probability a man with a net would appear and haul me off in a suit that buttons down the back.

But the ways of pure art are mysterious. Pittsburgh loved the drawings and some time later I received a Certificate of Excellence from the American Institute of Graphic Arts.

There is a reason people look the way they do. There seems to be no doubt that the face one wears has been earned through perseverance. Modern people are changing—they are becoming more standardized, they are getting to look more and more alike. The standardized storefront and the standardized face are related. The American, Frenchman, Italian, Englishman, and Russian are becoming indistinguishable. Not too many years ago a Soviet statesman looked like a Soviet statesman. Today, all statesmen look like Henry Cabot Lodge. The "look" sells the product. There is no longer any shock or surprise at discovering that a best-seller has been ghost-written and that the celebrated, accredited author is someone who "looks" good on TV—or at discovering that the voice in the singing title role of *My Fair Lady* was dubbed in to match the dumb *moues* of the ostensible star. These and other corruptions are considered perfectly normal. Even Presidents hire unelected writers to write their speeches for them. The resulting Presidents develop standard TV faces that are indistinguishable from the local dry cleaner's. There was a time when a President was capable of writing the Gettysburg Address all by himself, but that was a long time ago and he wound up looking like Lincoln. We are in an age where the individual is suspect, and in which the common aspiration is to "make it" as a cog. The uniformity of physical weight and height, the lack of face, the indifferent, modern, cool look does not readily lend itself to easy caricature.

Even the matinee idols, the grandiose heroes, burlesque comics, vamps, wheezing heavies, and booming actors of the not-too-distant past are fast disappearing. The calculated design of Marlene Dietrich's eyebrows, Mae West's sex, Greta Garbo's mouth, Mary Pickford's curls, Groucho's cigar, George M. Cohan's cane, Louis Armstrong's smile, Barrymore's profile, Eddie Cantor's eyes, Al Jolson's mouth, W. C. Fields' hat, Rudolph Valentino's nostrils, Bill "Bojangles" Robinson's teeth, Zazu Pitts' hands all had one thing in common—they were not for real. Their intention was not to imitate life at all—the very essence of stardom was unreal, extravagant, and artificial. The modern approach, however, demands a real, intelligent, serious person with whom one can identify. With rare exception, the names and faces of contemporary stars seem harder to remember and easier to forget. The documentary quality they strive for succeeds best when the star quality is unnoticed.

To isolate a particular actor into a special, one-of-a-kind, unmistakable "likeness" by means of abstract line is not made easier when the compliant actor, in his studied course of visual anonymity, wants to be lost in a pod like a pea. The problem is to avoid creating stereotyped drawings of stereotyped subjects. Pure stylization without content tends to be arid and lifeless and as a drawing system it could eventually destroy the artist. The temptation, in my own case, to imitate myself is a constant threat. When I get stuck, bored, or can no longer see with any conviction, I put the drawing aside. In time, the mental constipation disappears. Enthusiasm, assurance, and creative sight miraculously return—at least, that is the way the process has worked up until now.

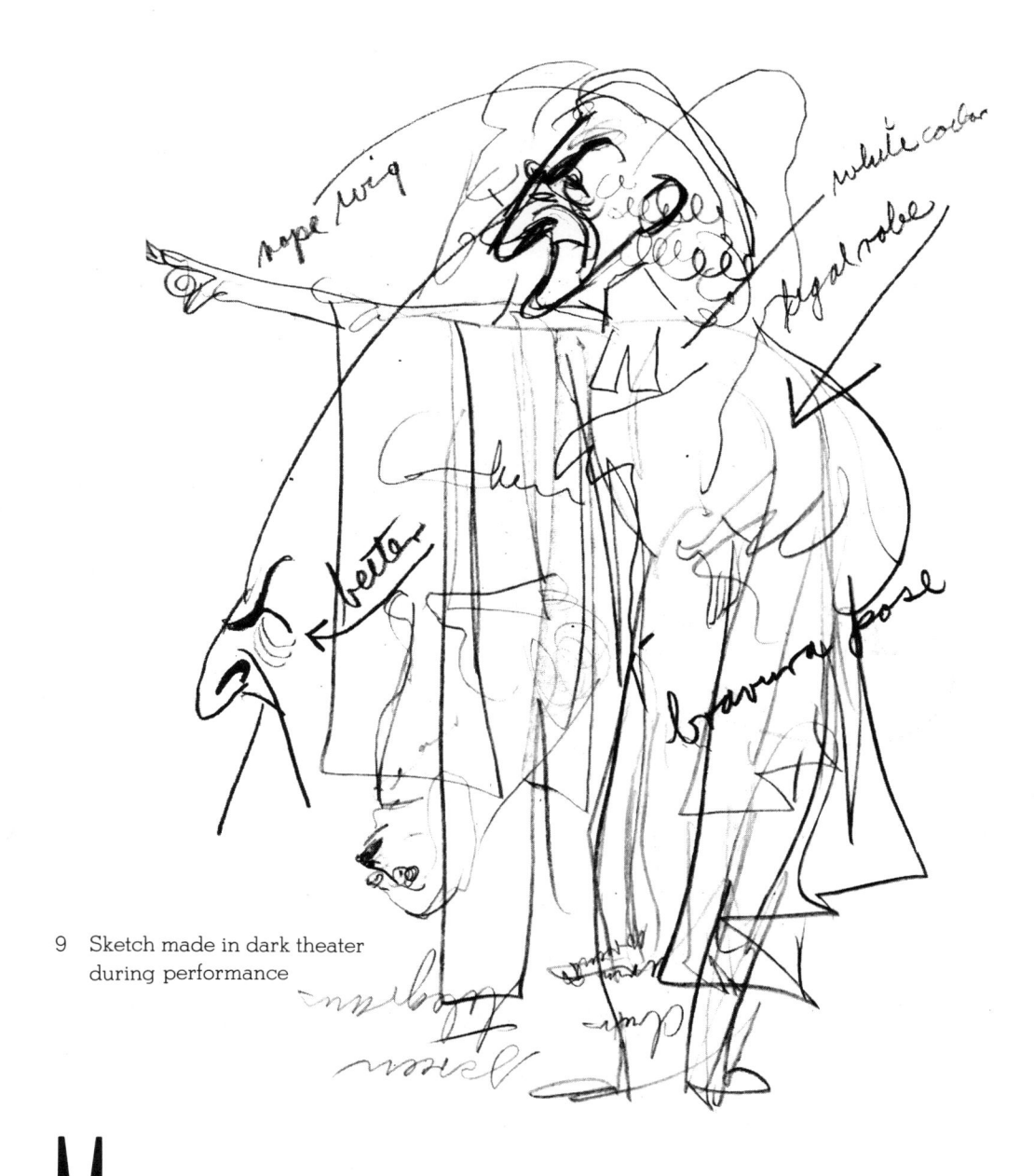

9 Sketch made in dark theater during performance

M y work has been mostly confined to the theater. One of the limitations in drawing caricatures of the theater is the darkness. When the house lights dim and the curtain rises, exposing the inevitable living room, the sketch pad had better be gripped securely, or the next few minutes will be spent groping in the dark trying to locate it. The only way to overcome this handicap is to learn to draw in the dark. I have practiced in complete darkness with a pencil stub and a small note pad, occasionally illuminating the pad with a flashlight to see if the scribbles made in the dark could be read. Using this process I eventually learned to draw in my pocket— a handy device for shy sitters. This system, a kind of shorthand employing written words and hieroglyphics, and which I alone can decipher, defeats the darkness. The coordination of transmitting images of the mind through the dexterity of the fingers may seem impossible, but concentrating on the image with great intensity and translating what is there into a drawing, without looking at the paper, is actually no more difficult to learn than professional typing. In a similar manner, many violinists perform with their eyes hermetically sealed, and it is not always essential for a pianist to see the keys in order to hit the right ones.

I studied sculpture, painting, drawing, and lithography at the National Academy, the Art Students League, and the London County Council. One of the instructors in one of these schools sagely advised, "Do not let the point of your pencil interfere with your artistic ability." This advice is probably the safest comment ever made about art, and I would not presume to improve on the observation. Equipped with sharpened pencils and a sketchbook, I catch an on-the-road performance of a show scheduled to open at a later date in New York. Seated out front on the aisle with a vacant seat next to me, I start sketching at the rise of the curtain. The sketches are illuminated with scribbled words describing action or detail too fleeting to draw. The visual memory is tricky and not always reliable; the words help to recapture the feeling experienced at the time.

One evening, returning from a tryout of *Fiddler on the Roof* in Boston, I discovered, from my sketches, that the vest worn by Zero Mostel buttoned the wrong way for a man. I phoned Boris Aronson, the show's designer, and asked whether my sketches were in error or were the men's clothes purposely designed that way. I could not understand why my sketches showed the vest buttoning the way it did. He assured me that in the period Sholom Aleichem was writing about there was no difference in the buttoning of coats worn by Jewish men and women—and yes, they were designed that way in the production. Having satisfied myself of the visual accuracy of this automatic recording, I went ahead with my drawing, leaving out this well-researched piece of costuming. I deliberately dressed Zero in a conventionally buttoned vest to avoid crank mail. Readers of caricature rarely write in praise of anything, but let an obvious error appear such as a fireplace without a flue, one too many stripes in a sergeant's chevrons, or, as in this case, a man wearing a vest buttoned the wrong way—even though the facts are correct—look out! The mail in this instance could have been staggering.

I recite this incident to point out the accuracy of unconsciously recorded observation—a collaboration of sight and hand, with no conscious thought at the

10   Zero Mostel in FIDDLER ON THE ROOF. 1964

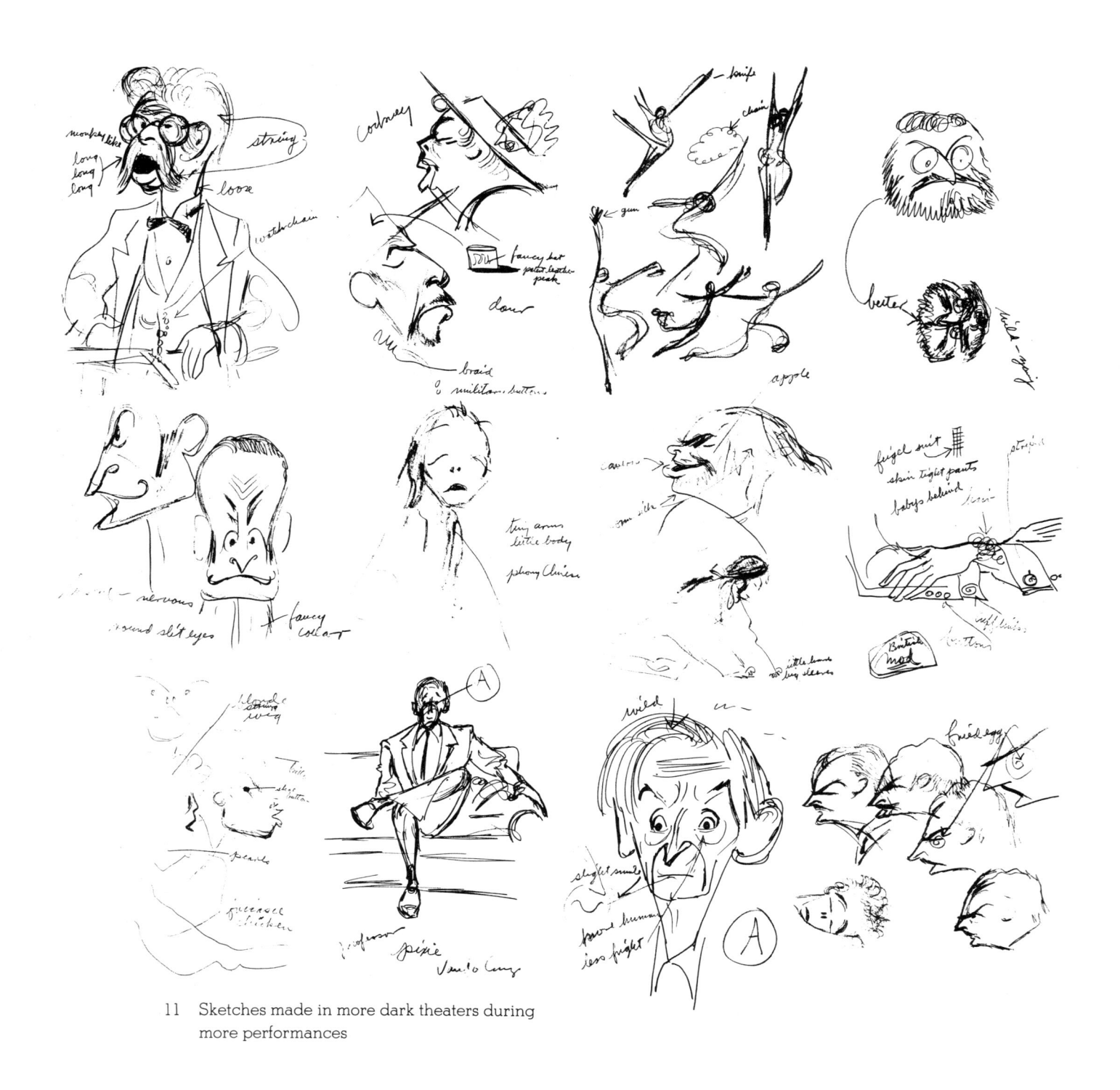

11 Sketches made in more dark theaters during more performances

controls. There it was—the eye saw it, the hand recorded it, and reason did not interfere. A similar phenomenon happens sometimes in capturing a likeness, the movement of a hand, the design of an eye, or a vest. The impression is conveyed to the paper by disciplined and continual practice. Once the curtain descends, the memory and the sketches combine to recreate the experience. A hasty glance at the sketches convinces, one way or the other, of their usefulness. If doubt persists, I hurry backstage to get the players in their dressing rooms before they take off their makeup and costumes. If, after these concentrated sittings, I still am not satisfied that I have captured the personality, I will make a careful, academic eye, ear, nose, and throat portrait. The realistic drawing helps to refresh my visual memory and avoid the pitfall of arid stylization.

Back in the studio with all my sketches and words scribbled during the performance, I correlate them into a designed composition for a finished caricature. Looking through old sketchbooks for the purpose of further clarifying this aspect of caricature, I find a hastily rendered sketch made in a darkened theater, perhaps twenty years ago, of a cadaverous actress with loose transparent skin; it has a notation alongside, with a scribbled arrow pointing to her arm. The words "fricassee chicken," legibly inscribed, bring back to mind the feeling about that arm that I wanted to get into my drawing. The sketch helped in recreating the shape of the arm, but "fricassee chicken" was the bones and muscle. Also helpful are such other notations as "leather hair," "exposed nerve," "idiot savant," "star," "spiral," "fried eggs," "bulb," "tomato," "sponge," or a marginal note "two holes," with an arrow pointing to a nose. Similarly indicated descriptions are of mouths as slits, pea holes, caverns, fangs; or of hair as corn silk, Brillo, rope, string, thread, fuzz, or cue ball. These abstractions are as clear to me as the sketch which accompanies them. The combination of the sketch and the word refreshes my visual memory, making it possible to combine the "seen" image and the "described" one into a unified drawing.

Working on a 20-by-30-inch triple-ply, cold-pressed illustration board, I use the whole board for one drawing, regardless of the size it eventually winds up in reproduction. A complicated drawing designed for an eight-column spread may have to be reduced to four columns flanked by overpowering dark photographs. The size of the reproduction as well as other last-minute decisions are dictated by editorial considerations over which I have no control. An important production whose opening date is switched at the last minute and should be accommodated on the first page of the drama section would cause a reshuffling or cutting of the drawing, stories, and news. The remake of the page is the editor's choice.

The most effective reproductions are those with the least reduction. One of the limitations in the primitive process of photoengraving is its inability to reproduce the width of a line as accurately as its length. The purposeful comments and accents resulting from varying widths of line lose their subtlety in mechanical distortion. The decision to be made is, which is the more important? The engraving? Or the drawing? If I were to make my drawings the same size as they are printed, the reproductions would be better, but the drawing itself would suffer by this restricting limitation. I prefer the freedom of expressing myself in a drawing, the size of the drawing determined only by the demands of the drawing. Sometimes I will start one and let it grow and grow until everything in it reaches an equally finished state of unfinishedness; by then it may be a very large drawing indeed, profuse in detail and complicated in design. Invariably, this type of ambitious drawing will suffer most in reproduction, for to reproduce it with any degree of fidelity would require two full pages of the Sunday *New York Times*. It comes as no surprise when the printed drawing, greatly reduced, appears like fly crap on the page. I have long ago given up the losing battle of layout.

The art of caricature, or rather the special branch of it that interests me, is not necessarily one of malice. It is never my aim to destroy the play or the actor by ridicule. My contribution is to take the character—created by the playwright and acted out by the actor—and reinvent it for the reader. The aim is to recreate the performed character and not reinterpret its "character" by ridicule or aggressive insult. The intent of the character portrayed on the stage is the "character" to be delineated in the drawing.

Unlike a political opponent whose inhuman policies I would want to destroy in the real world, my subject exists as fantasy in a world of make-believe. A drawing of an actor playing a character is a visual conviction of that character; but a political fathead, drawn as a fathead, is a political reality. As a matter of fact, the French equivalent for fathead is *poire*. The word became part of the French language in its secondary meaning as "fathead" rather than "pear" through its use in political caricature. Charles Philipon (editor of *La Caricature*, Paris, 1830) in four progressive stages drew *Le Roi bourgeois,* Louis Philippe, as a pear (*poire*). The drawings progressed from the initial realistic portrait of Louis Philippe into a slightly pear-shaped head; and in drawing number three the evolutionary process continued its inevitable destruction until the hair on the top of his head took on the shape and characteristics of a pear leaf; the final drawing was the complete fruit. Louis Philippe was the pear and the pear was Louis Philippe. The success of Philipon's caricature was immediate: he was brought to trial, condemned, and fined six thousand francs. His magazine subsequently published the text of the verdict on the cover, prominently displayed, as the law so prescribed. The full page was devoted to the decision handed down against him—the type was set to conform to the shape of a pear. For this bit of witty visual comment, Monsieur Philipon was hauled off to the Bastille to chuckle and enjoy the harvest of his sowing. This Machiavellian reward rarely comes to caricaturists anymore. A vicious caricature of today's "leader of men" may very well wind up inexpensively framed in the "leader's" living room. It is much more difficult nowadays to reach the nerve ends. The chore of coping with daily abuse and insult, both professionally and socially, along with the problems of toxic poisoning, taxes, and transportation, makes the caricature seem almost lovable by contrast. The caricature is accepted as a mark of esteem by one who has "made it"—an accolade of success, a sort of celebrity's passport.

It seems that everyone knows I always hide my daughter's name, NINA, in the designs of my drawings—in folds of sleeves, tousled hairdos, eyebrows, wrinkles, backgrounds, shoelaces—anywhere to make it difficult, but not too difficult, to find. This harmless insanity started quite innocently. It was the fall of 1945 and I was assigned to do a drawing for the cover of the Sunday *Times* drama page. The show was a musical entitled *Are You With It?* costarring Johnny Downs and Joan Roberts. I caught a matinee of this production in Philadelphia on the same day my darling wife, Dolly Haas, produced our daughter, Nina, in New York. Hurrying from the opening in Philadelphia to catch the one in New York, I arrived in time, with hours to spare. During those hours in the waiting room at Doctors Hospital, I nervously filled the remaining pages of my sketchbook with drawings of the conjured dark-haired girl my mother had been praying for.

All speculation ceased with the official announcement from the doctor. "Congratulations, sir, you're the father of a redheaded girl." After viewing our dog-tagged daughter through the glass wall, assuring myself that the full complement of toes and fingers were all in the right places, I returned to my studio to do the *Are You With It?* drawing as best I could under the circumstances. The musical had a circus background, which I used in my drawing. On an imagined poster, hung on the freak sideshow tent, I facetiously drew a newly born infant reading from a large book. Lettered on the poster, as billing, I printed "Nina the Wonder Child." Close friends and immediate family enjoyed a mild snicker over this infantile prank. And that is how it all began. Innocent enough?

But like those creatures on TV from outer space, who infest our living rooms with expanding flora and fauna, I, too, have been prey to an expanding audience beyond my control. Close friends have told other close friends that the name NINA is concealed in the *Times* drawing on Sunday, and the "game" has grown from a whisper to frightening proportions. Unfortunately I do not have the resources ("guts" may be the more apt word) to put an end to it. The first intimation that I had created a Frankenstein "indestructible" was the incredible response I received the first time I deliberately left Nina's name out of a drawing. Mail descended on me from all over, demanding, "Where is it?" "My wife says it's here in the feathers." "Our weekly pool cannot pay off without verification from you." "Is this it?" Each letter enclosed the printed reproduction with imagined NINAs circled on the drawing for positive identification. I next discovered that the photoengraving department at the *Times* had a pool of employees, each contributing a buck, winner take all, to the first one who spotted NINA in the engraved cut; which, as every sensible engraver knows, is seen backwards.

The next folly I committed was the unpardonable error of acceding to a request from my daughter to put her girl friend's name, LIZA, in a drawing. All hell broke loose when it appeared microscopically the following Sunday on the *Times* drama page. Flowers and telegrams arrived, one all the way from Alaska, congratulating my wife and me on the new arrival.

The next hair-raiser in this popular tidal wave was a note from Mr. Arthur Hays Sulzberger, publisher of the *Times:*

April 11, 1960

Dear Mr. Hirschfeld:

For some time now one of my first jobs in looking at our drama section is to find the name NINA. You see, my granddaughter went to school with your daughter and let me in on the secret. Last week I learned to my regret that occasionally there is more than one and that really isn't fair since not knowing how many there are leaves one with a sense of frustration.

Yours for only one NINA per Hirschfeld cartoon, I am

Faithfully yours,

Arthur Hays Sulzberger

In the same mail with Mr. Sulzberger's note there arrived another from a Mrs. Storrs of Cove Neck Road in Oyster Bay, New York. Forwarded to me from the drama desk at the *Times*, it read:

Dear Sirs:

Every other Sunday I have a delightful time trying to spot the NINAs of Mr. Hirschfeld's cartoon of the theatrical world. I am sure, however, that I miss some, especially since, for the last two issues, he has only had one to my knowledge. Would it be possible to ask him to put in the correct number in the corner somewhere? It would make Sundays much more relaxed for all five of us that challenge each other in the contest.

The game has given us a greater appreciation of the value of each line and detail in the drawing and has taught us considerably about the art of exaggeration, incidentally.

Very truly yours,

Mrs. Storrs

I dispatched this note to Mr. Sulzberger, and the next mail brought the following:

Dear Mr. Hirschfeld:

Thanks for your letter of the 16th. I'll look forward with interest to your "numbers racket"!
    I return Mrs. Storrs's letter herewith. I don't think I've ever before seen anyone sign a letter the way she did.
    With kind regards, I am

Faithfully yours,

Arthur Hays Sulzberger

A number appended to my signature, denoting the exact number of NINAs in the drawing, has appeared ever since. The Chicago *Sun Times,* the St. Louis *Post Dispatch,* news syndicates, columnists, *Life, Look,* and a flock of other magazines, as well as television, have blown up this innocent gesture heralding the arrival of our daughter into an internationally famous game. The self-expanding force of mass media eventually reached into the impenetrable inner circle of the Pentagon in Washington. A Pentagon communiqué addressed to me from Air Force headquarters requested permission to use my drawings as part of the curriculum in their student aviation training course. Blowups of the drawings were to be shown on a full-size movie screen, and the student pilots would be required to ferret out the NINAs in the projected drawing. Grading would be based on the speed with which the pilots located the NINA targets. Looking back on that fateful day in 1945 when I innocently put Nina's name in the *Are You With It?* drawing, it never occurred to me that twenty years later I would be asked permission to use this foolish prank to help our pilots pinpoint targets around the world.

12 "Nina's Revenge." This is Nina, with no NINAs concealed in the drawing. There are, however, two ALs and two DOLLYs (the names of her wayward parents) to help keep the drawing and national sanity in balance. 1964

Every age in the history of man's slow progress to oblivion has produced its own standard of beauty. From the classic proportions of the heroic Greek goddess to the underpowering Twiggy, man has invented his own ideal to suit his own time. Everyone will agree that a tintype of a corseted, buxom, balloon-breasted sexpot of the 1890's is funny and artificial when compared to a color photograph of a sleek bikini-clad Lolita of the 1980's lolling on a sunny beach. To the caricaturist, both produce distortions of reality capable of inducing laughter or beauty, or both. The universal recognition that our generation is brighter and prettier than our parents' generation is obvious—just as it was when our parents recognized that their generation was brighter and prettier than their parents' generation, who . . . etc.
I do not mean to imply that the caricaturist is not subject to the same unreasonable sense of superiority or that he misses the humor of the tintype; I merely insist that the caricaturist must also see the humor in the photo of the contemporary beauty just as clearly. "Beauty" is a dangerous word. "Love" is another beaut. "Art" is pretty good, too. But "Caricature". . . well, that's about as impossible as one can get. I have never been able to convince anyone of the simple fact that Caricature and Beauty are really the same to a caricaturist. Beauty may be the beaded lash growing out of an eyelid or the hair growing out of an ear. It may be the perfectly formed female figure; but it does not have to be—it could be an infected wart. The lover whose nostrils dilate at the sight of his lady fair's upraised arm is not considered eccentric in Hungary. He is enticed by exquisitely groomed ladies who cultivate small hair mattresses under their arms. This national affliction is perfectly normal for Hungary. A French *homme fatal* finds his lady friend's mustache irresistible.
A young girl with a lower lip capable of holding a steak platter is a Ubangi chief's dream. Each country has invented its own national concept of beauty. But all would agree (apart from local idiosyncrasies) that a beautiful woman, perfectly formed, is a cherished thing of beauty. And that a female crocodile or cockroach, perfectly formed, is a revolting thing of ugliness. That is, all would agree, except a male crocodile or cockroach . . . and perhaps a few caricaturists.

A.H.

EARLY LITHOGRAPHS

13   Soviet worker, Moscow. 1927

14   The Dizzy Club. 1931

15 Public bar. 1931

16   La Serviette au Cou. 1931

17 "Peace in Our Time"—Neville Chamberlain. 1939

THEATER

18 Basil Rathbone in THE COMMAND TO LOVE. 1928

19 Mary Martin in SOUTH PACIFIC. 1949

20   Left to right: Douglas Deane, Tom Pedi, Stubby Kaye, Johnny Silver, Robert Alda, Sam Levene, B. S. Pully, Vivian Blaine, Pat Rooney, Sr., and Isabel Bigley in GUYS AND DOLLS. 1950

21 Bette Davis in TWO'S COMPANY. 1952

22 Celeste Holm in INVITATION TO A MARCH. 1960

23 Anne Jackson, Michael Wager, Viveca Lindfors, George Voskovec, and Dane Clark, seated in front of a picture of Bertold Brecht, listen to Lotte Lenya sing in BRECHT ON BRECHT. 1962

24 Peter Cook, Jonathan Miller, Alan Bennett, and Dudley Moore interpret Shakespeare in BEYOND THE FRINGE. 1962

25 Barbra Streisand, who portrayed Fanny Brice in FUNNY
    GIRL, is juxtaposed with a 1910 photograph of the late
    comedienne. 1964

26 Peter Ustinov in PHOTO FINISH, which he also wrote and directed. 1963

27 Veronica Tyler, William Warfield, and Ralph Guillaume in PORGY AND BESS. 1964

28 Josephine Baker appears in New York after many years in France. 1964

29 Walter Matthau and Art Carney in THE ODD COUPLE. 1965

30 Gwen Verdon, flanked by Helen Gallagher and Thelma Oliver in a dance scene from SWEET CHARITY. 1966

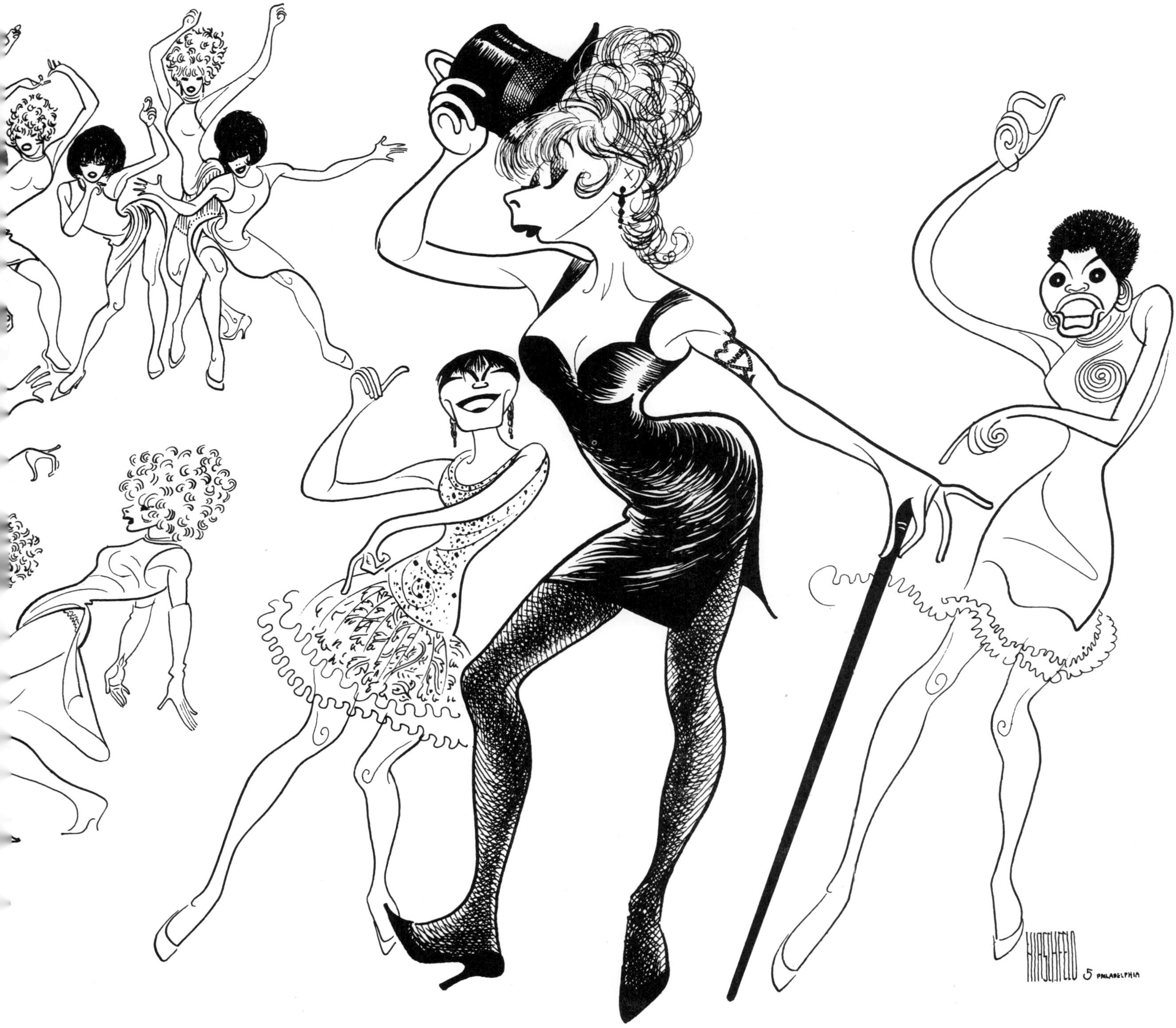
HIRSCHFELD
5 PHILADELPHIA

31   Mary Martin and Robert Preston in I DO! I DO! 1966

32 Beatrice Arthur, Angela Lansbury, and Jane Connell in MAME. 1966

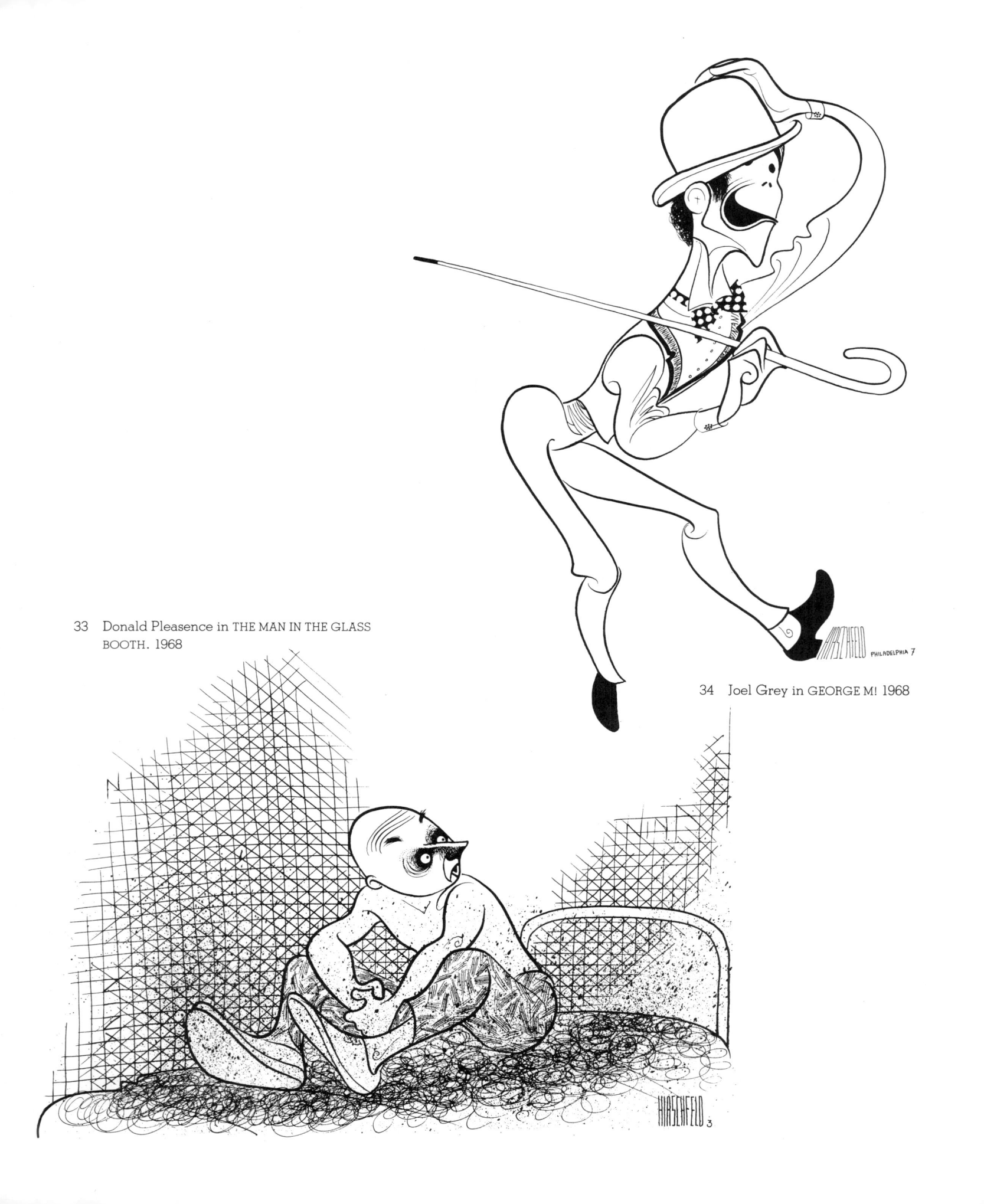

33 Donald Pleasence in THE MAN IN THE GLASS BOOTH. 1968

34 Joel Grey in GEORGE M! 1968

35 Julie Harris in FORTY CARATS. 1968

36 Jason Robards, Jr. and Diana Sands in
WE BOMBED IN NEW HAVEN. 1968

37 James Coco in THE TRANSFIGURATION OF BENNO BLIMPIE. 1976

38 Tom Courtenay in OTHERWISE ENGAGED. 1976

39 Eartha Kitt in TIMBUKTU!, the musical version of KISMET. 1978

40   Melba Moore in TIMBUKTU! 1978

41 Jean Marsh in WHOSE LIFE IS IT ANYWAY? 1978

42 Gilda Radner of television's SATURDAY NIGHT LIVE as Lisa Loopner in her Broadway revue, LIVE FROM NEW YORK. 1979

43   John Lithgow in BEDROOM FARCE. 1979

44   Mildred Natwick in BEDROOM FARCE. 1979

45   Gregory Hines in COMIN' UPTOWN. 1979

46   Maggie Smith in Tom Stoppard's NIGHT AND DAY. 1979

47   Mia Farrow and Anthony Perkins in ROMANTIC COMEDY. 1979

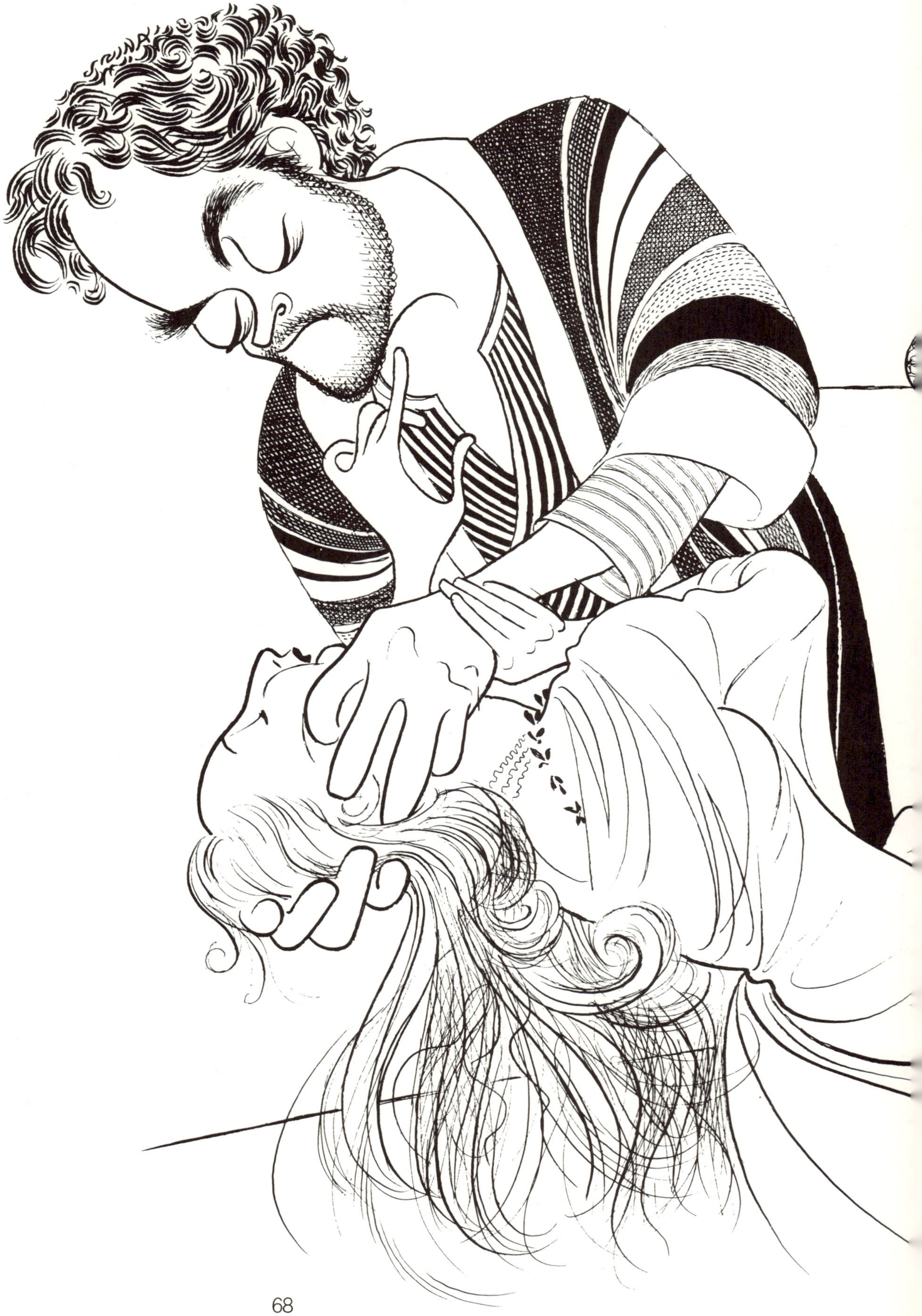

48 Raul Julia, Frances Conroy, and Richard Dreyfuss in
The New York Shakespeare Festival's production of
OTHELLO at the Delacorte Theater in Central Park.
1979

49   Dee Dee Bridgewater in
     THE 1940'S RADIO HOUR.
     1979

50   Ann Miller in
     SUGAR BABIES. 1979

51 Anne Twomey in NUTS. 1980

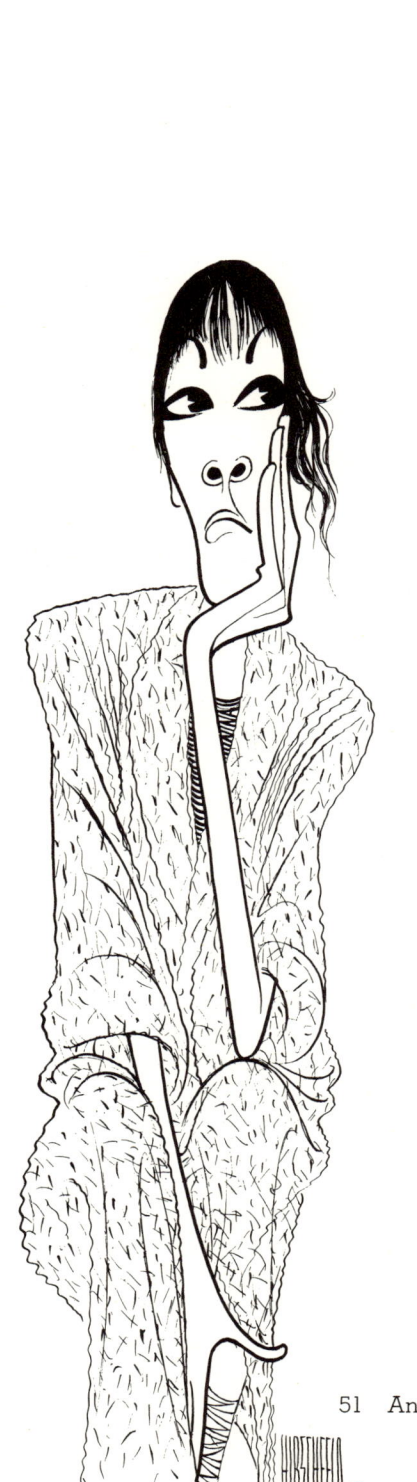

52 Daniel Seltzer in Samuel Beckett's ENDGAME. 1980

53 Jim Dale in BARNUM. 1980

54 Foreground, left to right: Lois DeBanzi, Elizabeth Wilson, and Maureen O'Sullivan. Background, left to right: Gary Merrill, David Rounds, Nancy Marchand, Teresa Wright, Richard Hamilton, and Maurice Copeland in MORNING'S AT SEVEN. 1980

55 Judd Hirsch and Trish Hawkins in TALLEY'S FOLLY. 1980

56   George Hearn in WATCH ON THE RHINE. 1980

57 Jerry Orbach in 42nd STREET. 1980

58 W. C. Fields in the film short THE BARBERSHOP.
   1933. (Drawing done in 1975.)

59 Charles Laughton and Clark Gable in MUTINY ON THE BOUNTY. 1935

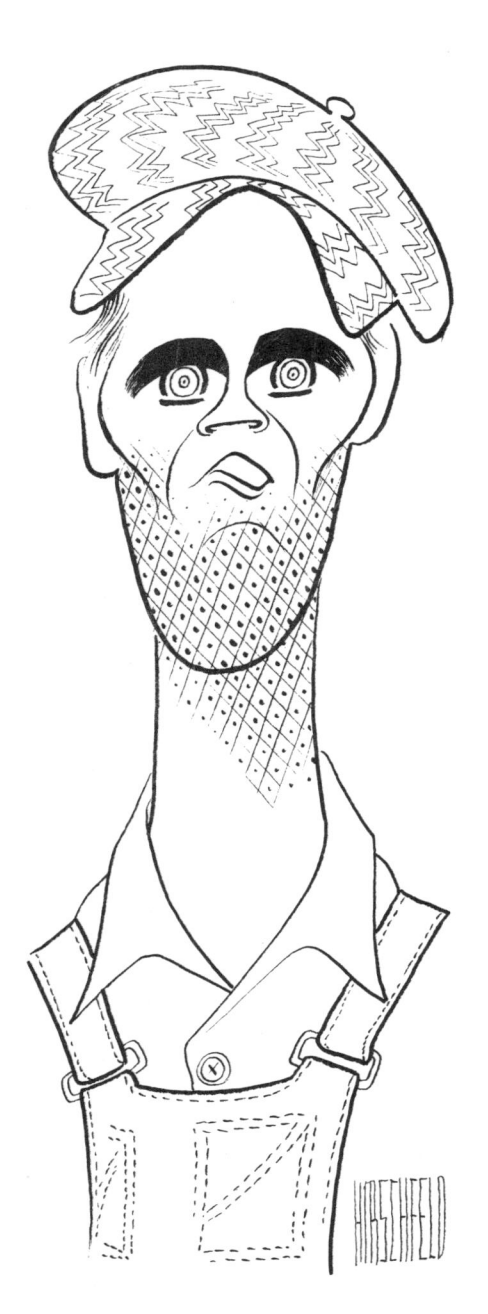

60 Henry Fonda in THE GRAPES OF WRATH. 1940.
(Drawing done for television advertisement in 1978.)

61 Erich von Stroheim and Gloria Swanson in Billy Wilder's SUNSET BOULEVARD. 1950

62 Gene Kelly in SINGIN' IN THE RAIN. 1952

63   Grace Kelly and Bing Crosby in THE COUNTRY GIRL. 1954

64   Eva Marie Saint and Marlon Brando in
ON THE WATERFRONT. 1954

65 Judy Garland in A STAR IS BORN. 1954

66 Cary Grant in Alfred Hitchcock's TO CATCH A THIEF. 1955. (Drawing done for television advertisement in 1978.)

67 Melina Mercouri and Jules Dassin in NEVER ON SUNDAY. 1958

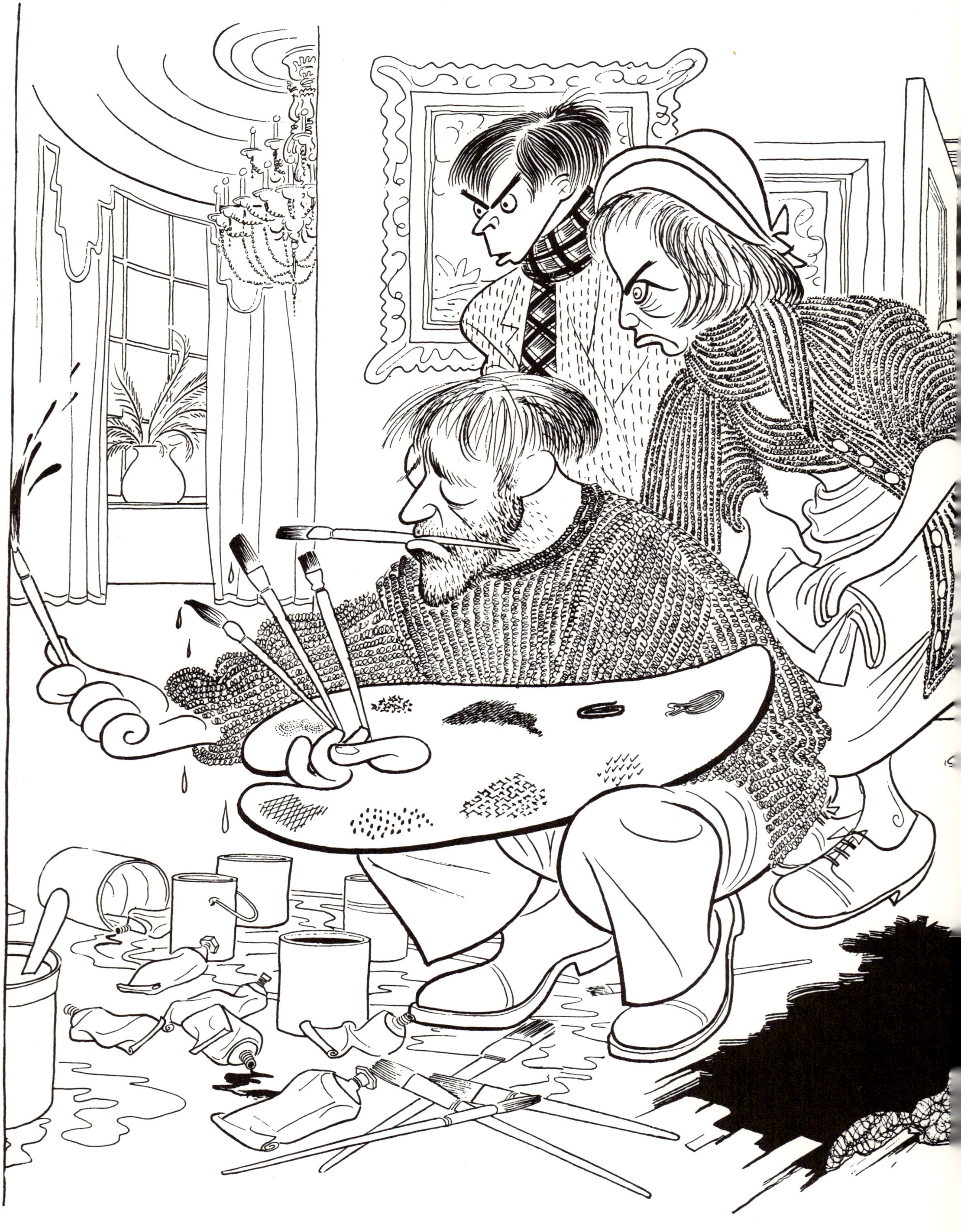

68 Alec Guinness, Mike Morgan, Kay Walsh, and Michael Gough, in THE HORSE'S MOUTH, unaware that the startled owners of the apartment (in background) have unexpectedly returned. 1958

69 Spencer Tracy in THE OLD MAN AND THE SEA. 1958

70 Tony Curtis, Marilyn Monroe, and Jack Lemmon in SOME LIKE IT HOT. 1959

71   Paul Muni in THE LAST ANGRY MAN. 1959

72 Jack Lemmon and Shirley MacLaine in THE APARTMENT. 1960

73 Foreground, left to right: Spencer Tracy and Fredric March. Background, left to right: Gene Kelly, Donna Anderson, Dick York, and Harry Morgan in INHERIT THE WIND. 1960

74 As a chill wind swept in off the Hudson River, co-directors Robert Wise (left) and Jerome Robbins (right) screen-tested a group of dancers on New York's West Side for the film version of WEST SIDE STORY. 1960

75 Claudia McNeil and Sidney Poitier in A RAISIN IN THE SUN. 1961.
    (Drawing done for television advertisement in 1978.)

76 Montgomery Clift, Marilyn Monroe, and Clark Gable
    in THE MISFITS. 1961

77 Anne Bancroft and Patty Duke in THE MIRACLE WORKER. 1962

78 Shirley MacLaine and Robert Mitchum in
TWO FOR THE SEESAW. 1962

79   Bob Hope and Bing Crosby in THE ROAD TO HONG KONG. 1962

80 Fred Astaire in ROYAL WEDDING. 1962

81 On the set during the shooting of IRMA LA DOUCE, director Billy Wilder demonstrates to Shirley MacLaine the proper stance of a Parisian hooker, while Jack Lemmon looks on. 1963

82 Counterclockwise: Richard Burton, Ava Gardner, Sue Lyon, Deborah Kerr, and Cyril Delvanti in THE NIGHT OF THE IGUANA. 1964

83 Simone Signoret, Lee Marvin, Oskar Werner, Vivien Leigh, Heinz Ruehmann, José Ferrer, and Michael Dunn in SHIP OF FOOLS. 1965

84   Alec Guinness, Geraldine Chaplin, Ralph Richardson, and Omar Sharif in DOCTOR ZHIVAGO. 1965

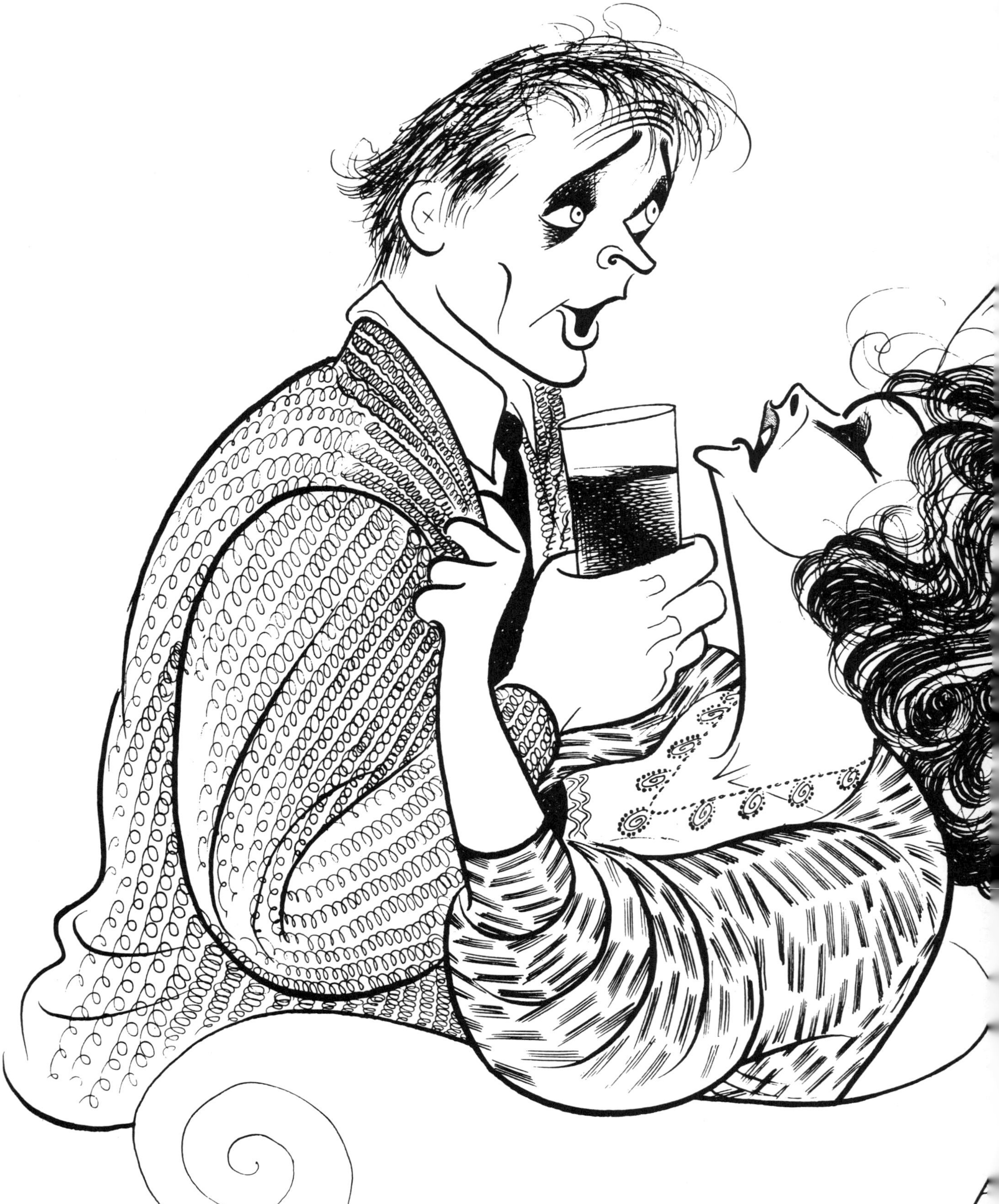

85 Richard Burton, Elizabeth Taylor, George Segal, and Sandy Dennis in WHO'S AFRAID OF VIRGINIA WOOLF? 1966

86 Alan Bates, Julie Christie, Peter Finch, and Terence Stamp in FAR FROM THE MADDING CROWD. 1967

87 Spencer Tracy, Katharine Hepburn, Katherine Houghton, and Sidney Poitier in GUESS WHO'S COMING TO DINNER? 1968

88 Julie Christie and Warren Beatty in McCABE AND MRS. MILLER. 1971

89 Eileen Heckart, Edward Albert, and Goldie Hawn in BUTTERFLIES ARE FREE. 1972

90 Glenda Jackson and George Segal in
    A TOUCH OF CLASS. 1973

91 Jack Lemmon and Anne Bancroft in THE PRISONER OF SECOND AVENUE. 1975

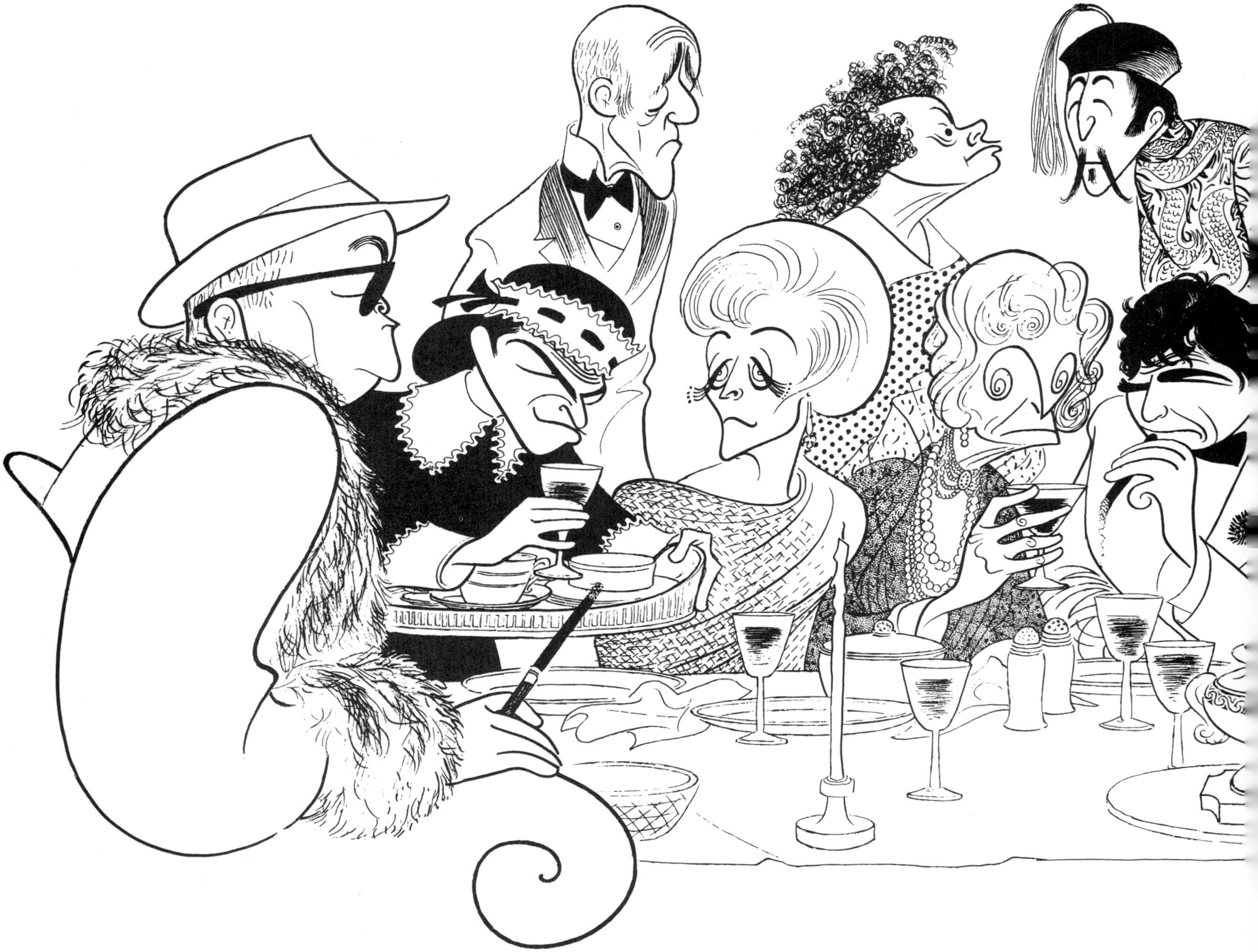

92 Foreground, left to right: Truman Capote, Nancy Walker, Maggie Smith, Estelle Winwood, Peter Falk, Eileen Brennan, James Coco, and David Niven. Background, left to right: Alec Guinness, Elsa Lanchester, and Peter Sellers in MURDER BY DEATH. 1976

93 Laurence Olivier, Kate Nelligan, and Frank Langella in DRACULA. 1979

94 Lee Strasberg, George Burns, and Art Carney in GOING IN STYLE. 1979

95 Marsha Mason and James Caan in Neil Simon's CHAPTER TWO. 1979

96   Chevy Chase, Goldie Hawn, and Charles Grodin in IT SEEMS LIKE OLD TIMES. 1980

PERSONALITIES

97 The Marx Brothers: Harpo, Chico, and Groucho. Cotton, steel wool, fur, and pen and ink. 1935

98   Laurel and Hardy. Fabric, pen and ink, and watercolor. c. 1935

99 Franklin Delano Roosevelt. 1944

100 Marian Anderson. 1948

101 Sean O'Casey. c. 1953

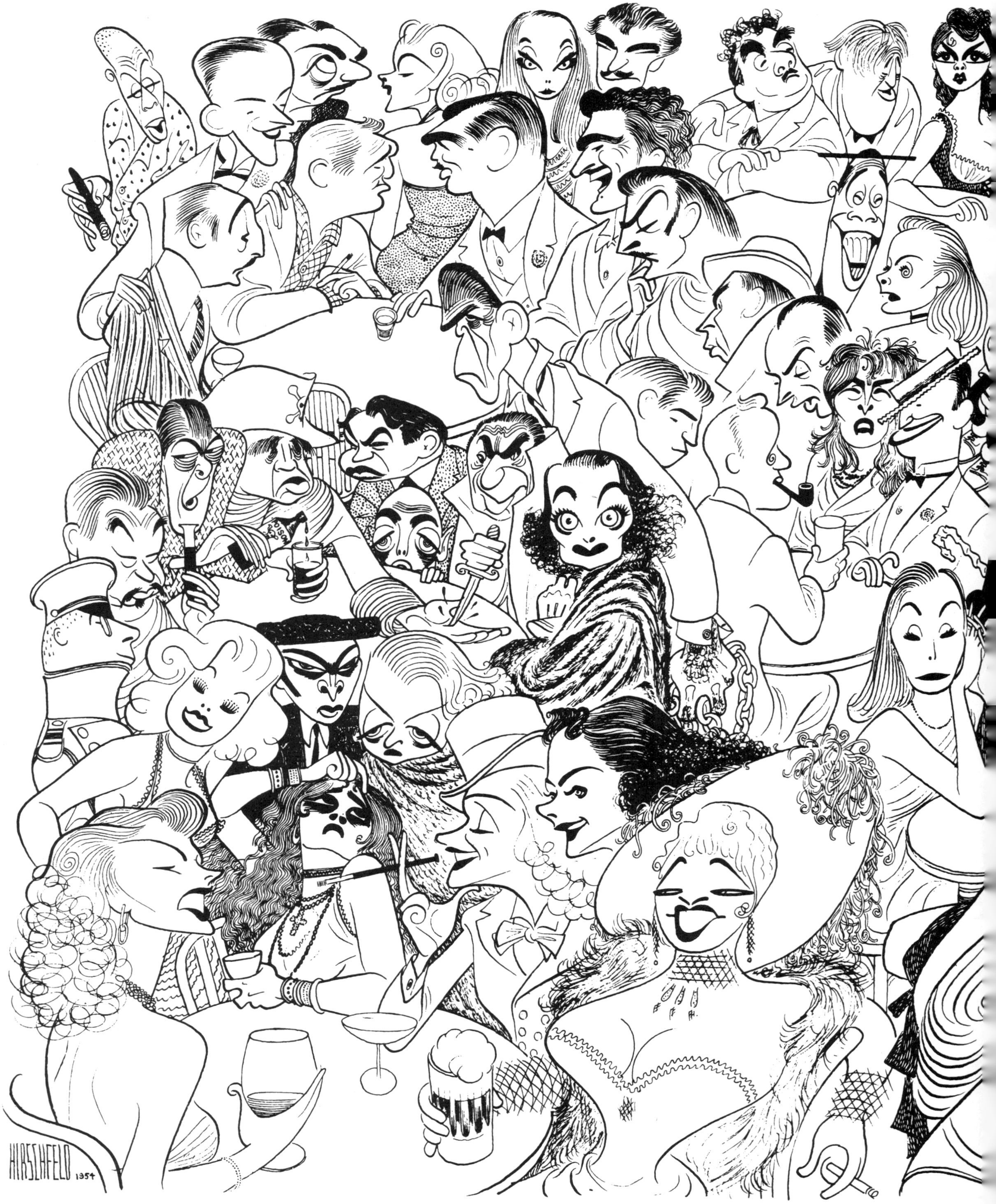
HIRSCHFELD 1954

102 The Movies. 1954. See page 159 for identifications

103 Ed Wynn. 1959

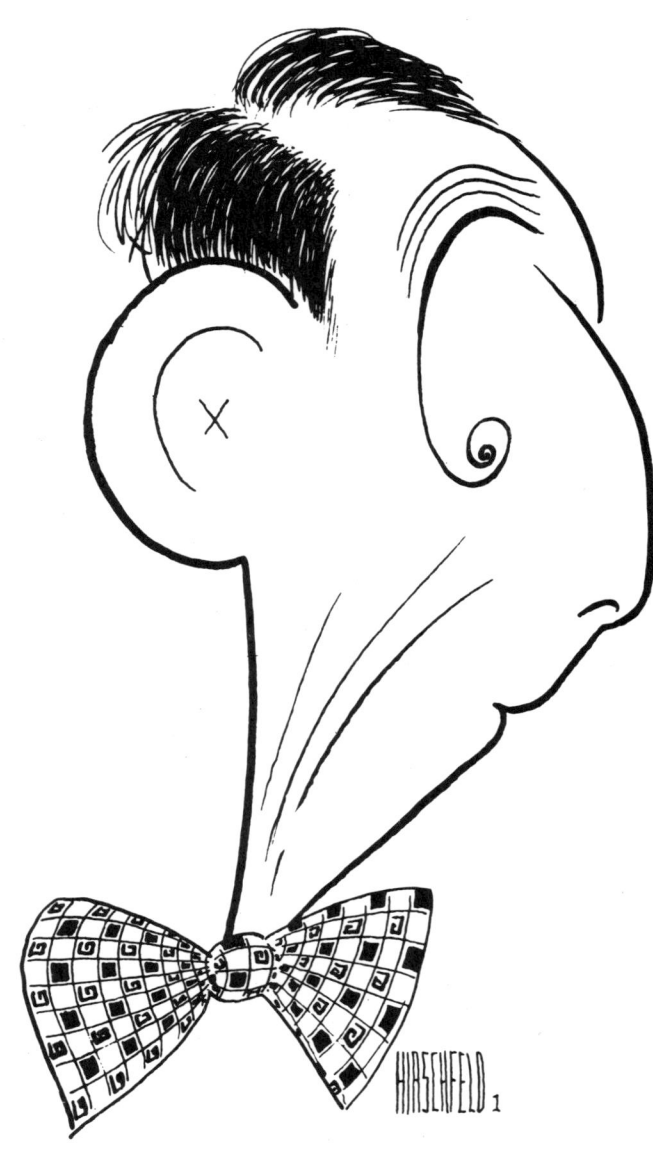

104 Ray Bolger. 1959

105 Jack Paar. 1961

106 Bertrand Russell. 1961

107 Lauren Bacall. 1962

108 The famous wits of the Algonquin Round Table. Clockwise, left foreground: Robert Sherwood, Dorothy Parker, Robert Benchley, Alexander Woollcott, Heywood Broun, Marc Connelly, Franklin P. Adams, Edna Ferber, and George S. Kaufman. Background, left to right: Lynn Fontanne, Alfred Lunt, Frank Crowninshield, and host Frank Case. 1962

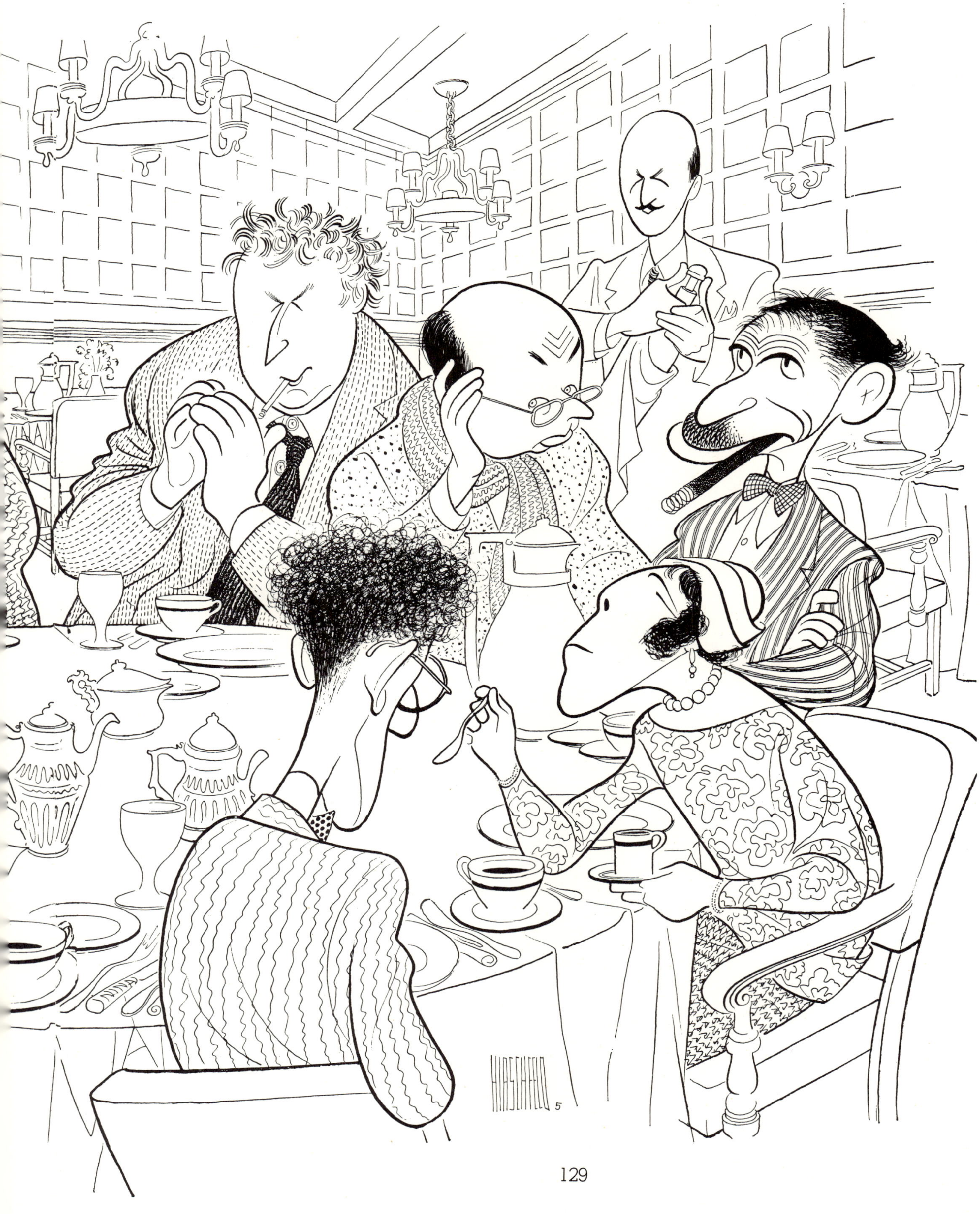
HIRSCHFELD

109 Walter Cronkite. 1963

110 Jack Benny. 1963

130

111 Red Skelton. 1963

112 Victor Borge. 1963

113 Ed Sullivan. 1963

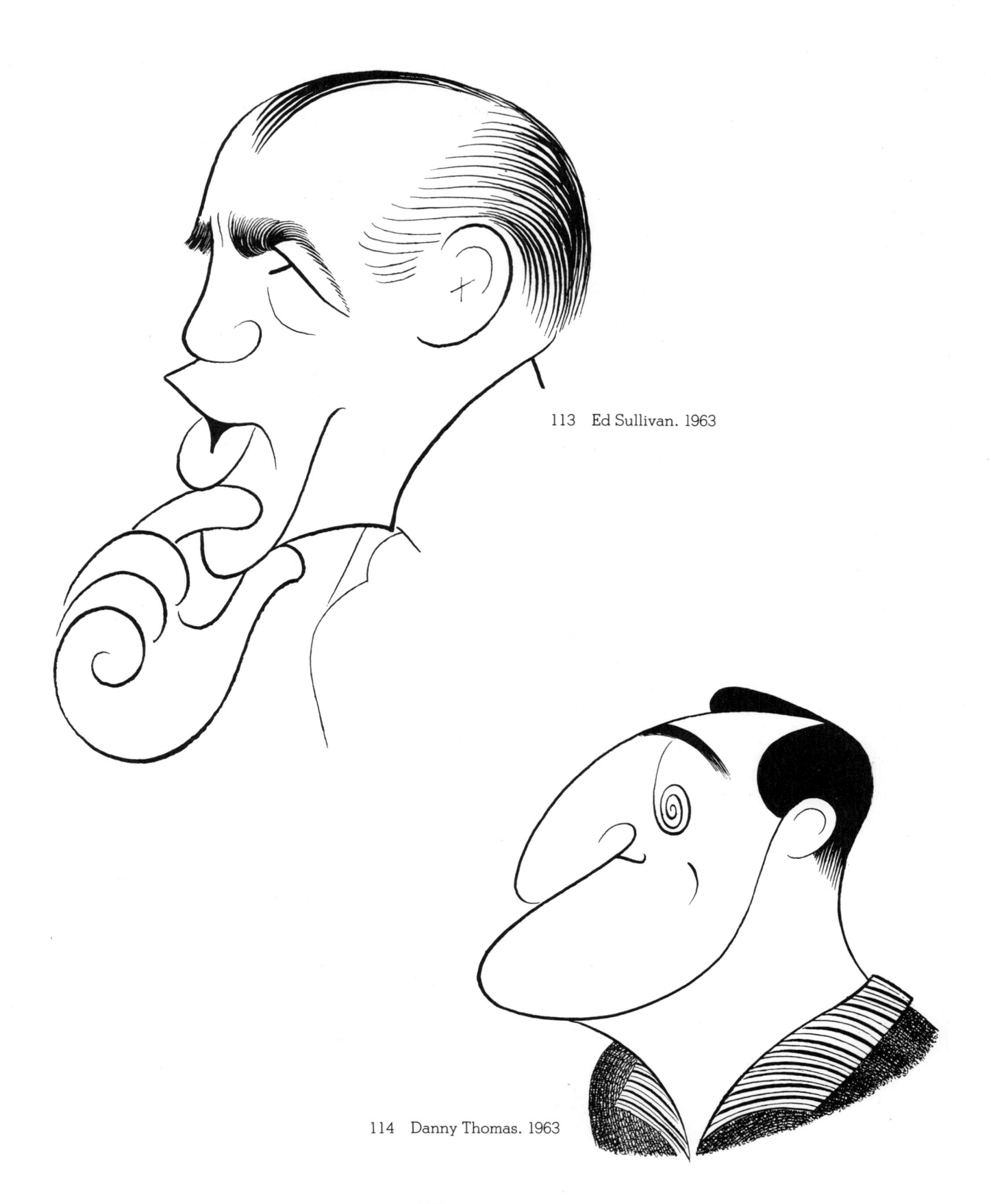

114 Danny Thomas. 1963

115 Terry Thomas. 1963

116 Boris Karloff. 1963

117 Danny Kaye. 1963

118 Judy Garland. 1963

119 Maurice Chevalier. 1963

120 Unlikely Casting: Barry Goldwater and Lyndon Johnson in WAITING FOR GODOT. 1964

121 More Unlikely Casting: Robert Preston and Sammy Davis, Jr. as the Dromio Twins in THE BOYS FROM SYRACUSE. 1964

122 Pearl Bailey and Carol Channing, Broadway's most famous "Dollys," together in a television special. 1969

123 Leonard Bernstein. 1967

124 Tallulah Bankhead in her dressing room backstage at the Booth Theatre. 1965

125 Elvis Presley in concert. 1969

126 Woody Allen. 1973

127 S. J. Perelman. c. 1974

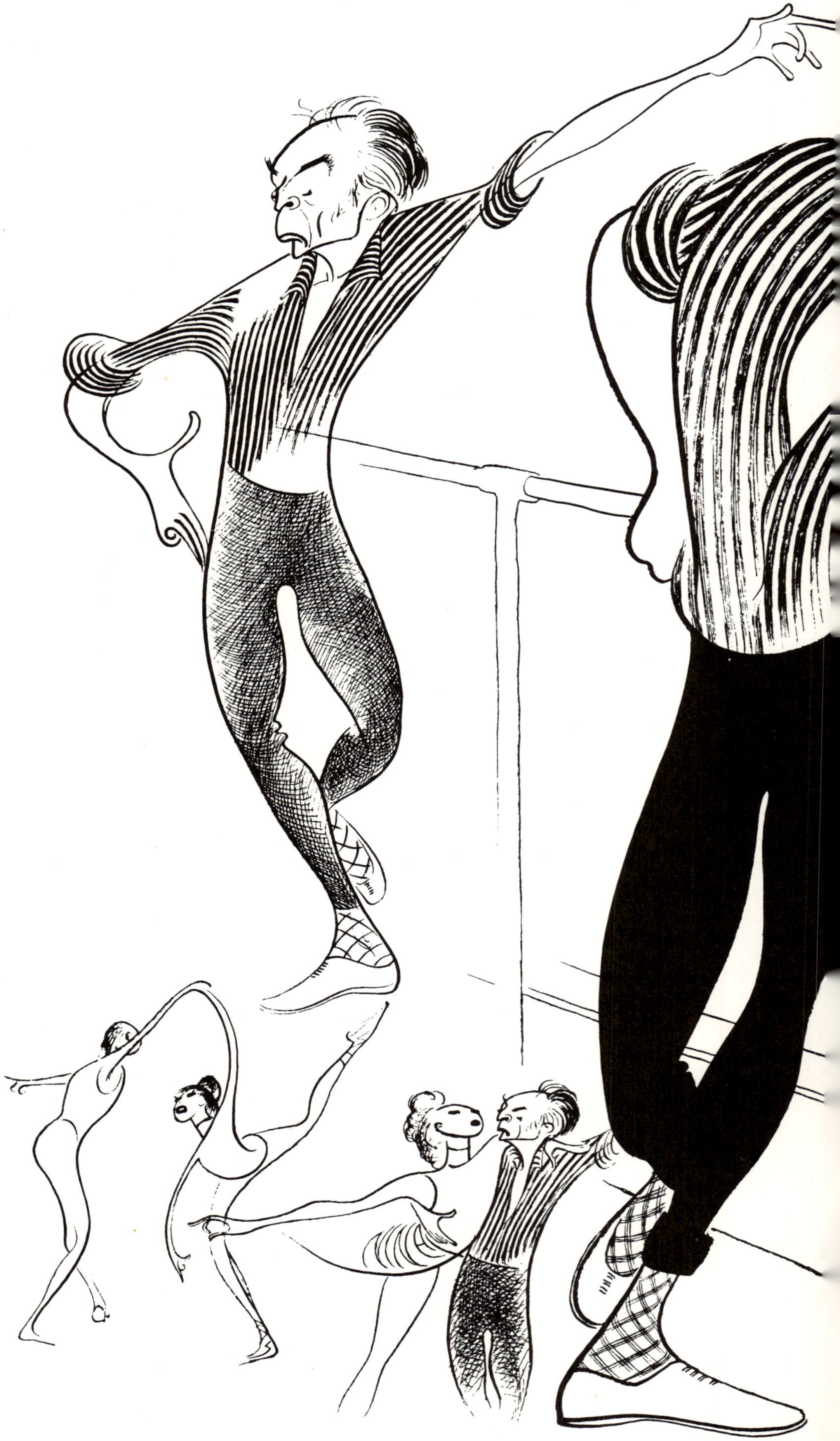

128 A celebration of George Balanchine. 1974

129 The Marx Brothers: Chico, Groucho, and Harpo. 1974

130 Lina Wertmuller. 1980

131 Richard Benjamin. 1975

132 Tennessee Williams and Arthur Miller. 1975

133 Playwrights at Work. Clockwise, lower left to right: Edward Albee, Jack Gelber, Jack Richardson, and Arthur Kopit. 1977

134 Kenny Rogers. 1980

135 Cinderella at the Palace, a television special. Clockwise, upper left to right:
Tom Jones, Andy Williams, Paul Anka, Ann-Margret, Gene Kelly,
Sammy Davis, Jr., Marlene Ricci, and (center) Frank Sinatra. 1979

136 John Chancellor and David Brinkley. Advertisement for NBC News 1980 Convention Coverage. 1980

PORTRAIT OF THE ARTIST

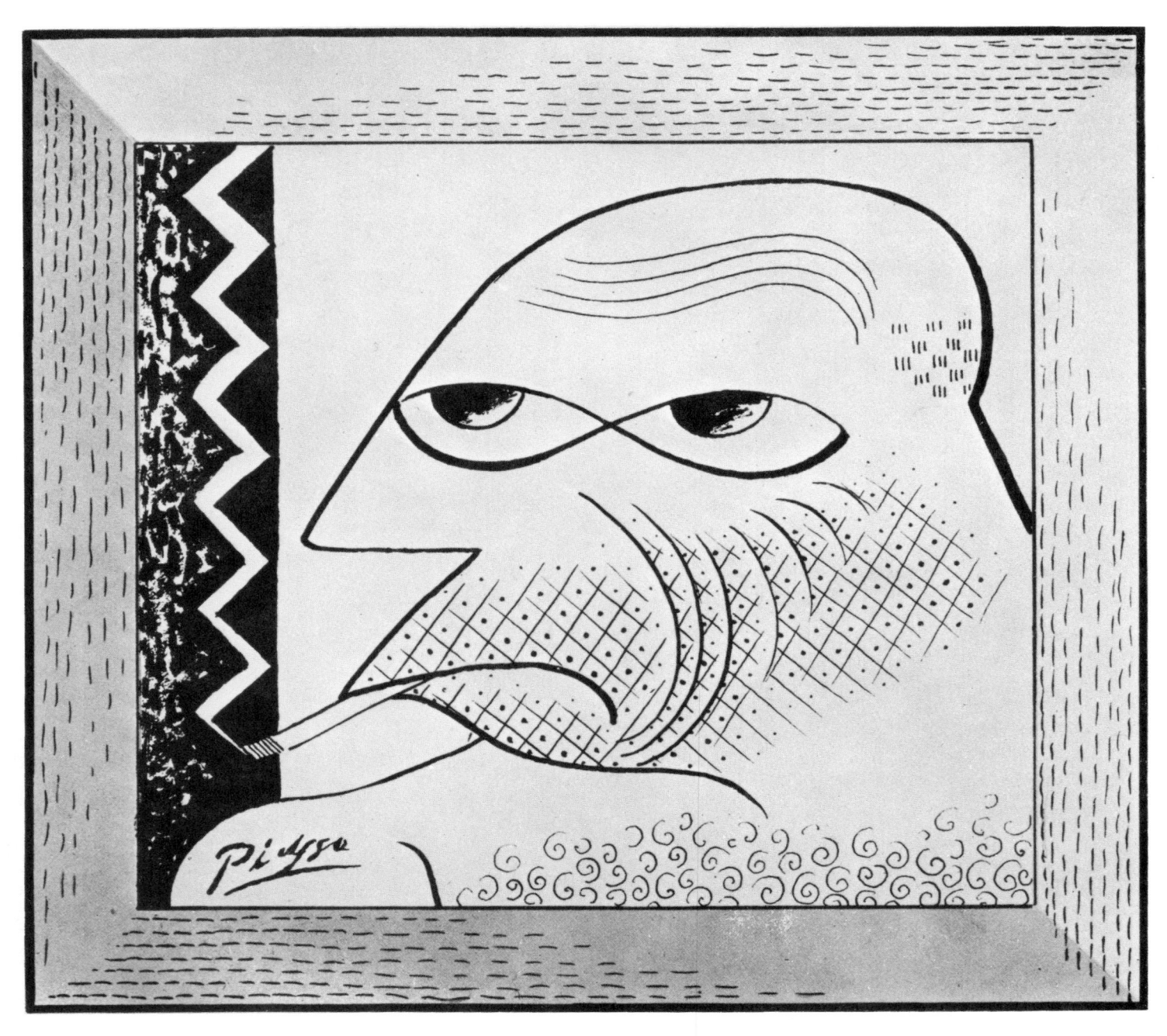

137   Pablo Picasso. 1961

138 Henri Matisse. 1961

139 Marc Chagall. 1961

140   Salvador Dali. 1961

141   The Connoisseurs. 1963

INDEX

Adams, Franklin P. 128–29
Albee, Edward 149
Albert, Edward 109
Alda, Robert 45
Algonquin Round Table 128–29
ALL AMERICAN 21
Allen, Woody 143
Anderson, Donna 92
Anderson, Marian 120
Anka, Paul 151
Ann-Margret 151
APARTMENT, THE 91
Arthur, Beatrice 57
Astaire, Fred 99

Bacall, Lauren 127
Bailey, Pearl 140
Baker, Josephine 53
Balanchine, George 144–45
Bancroft, Anne 96–97, 111
Bankhead, Tallulah 141
BARBERSHOP, THE 78
BARNUM 72
Bates, Alan 106
Beatty, Warren 108
BEDROOM FARCE 65
Benchley, Robert 128–29
Benjamin, Richard 147
Bennett, Alan 49
Benny, Jack 130
Bernstein, Leonard 141
BEYOND THE FRINGE 49
Bigley, Isabel 45
Blaine, Vivian 45
Bolger, Ray 19, 20–21, 124
Borge, Victor 132
BOYS FROM SYRACUSE, THE 139
Brando, Marlon 82
Brecht, Bertold 48
BRECHT ON BRECHT 48
Brennan, Eileen 112–13
Brice, Fanny 50
Bridgewater, Dee Dee 70
Brinkley, David 152
Broun, Heywood 128–29
Burns, George 115
Burton, Richard 101, 104–5
BUTTERFLIES ARE FREE 109

Caan, James 115
Capote, Truman 112–13
Carney, Art 54, 115
Case, Frank 128–29
Chagall, Marc 156
Chamberlain, Neville 42
Chancellor, John 152
Change-of-address card 16
Channing, Carol 19, 21, 140
Chaplin, Charlie 17–20
Chaplin, Geraldine 103

CHAPTER TWO 115
Chase, Chevy 116
Chevalier, Maurice 137
Christie, Julie 106, 108
Cinderella at the Palace 151
Clark, Dane 48
Clift, Montgomery 95
Coco, James 60, 112–13
COMIN' UPTOWN 66
COMMAND TO LOVE, THE 44
Connell, Jane 57
Connelly, Marc 128–29
Connoisseurs, The 158
Conroy, Frances 68–69
Cook, Peter 49
Copeland, Maurice 73
COUNTRY GIRL, THE 82
Courtenay, Tom 60
Cronkite, Walter 130
Crosby, Bing, 19, 82, 98
Crowninshield, Frank 128–29
Curtis, Tony 88–89

Dale, Jim 72
Dali, Salvador 157
Dassin, Jules 85
Davis, Bette 46
Davis, Sammy, Jr. 19, 139, 151
Deane, Douglas 45
DeBanzi, Lois 73
Delvanti, Cyril 101
Dennis, Sandy 104–5
Dizzy Club, The 39
DOCTOR ZHIVAGO 103
DRACULA 114
Dreyfuss, Richard 68–69
Duke, Patty 96–97
Dunn, Michael 102

ENDGAME 71

Falk, Peter 112–13
FAR FROM THE MADDING CROWD 106
Farrow, Mia 67

The Movies. (see pages 122–23)

1 Rita Hayworth
2 Jean Harlow
3 Theda Bara
4 Rudolph Valentino
5 Bette Davis
6 Marlene Dietrich
7 Hedy Lamarr
8 Mae West
9 Greta Garbo
10 Lillian Gish
11 Dorothy Gish
12 Gloria Swanson
13 Mary Pickford
14 Douglas Fairbanks
15 Katharine Hepburn
16 Shirley Temple
17 Norma Shearer
18 Gary Cooper
19 Ingrid Bergman
20 William S. Hart
21 Ben Turpin
22 Clara Bow
23 Harold Lloyd
24 Harry Langdon
25 Charlie Chaplin
26 Buster Keaton
27 Oliver Hardy
28 Stan Laurel
29 Mickey Rooney
30 W. C. Fields
31 Jimmy Durante
32 Bing Crosby
33 Bob Hope
34 Judy Garland
35 Marilyn Monroe
36 George Arliss
37 Orson Welles
38 Marie Dressler
39 Wallace Beery
40 Chico Marx
41 Groucho Marx
42 Harpo Marx
43 Mickey Mouse
44 Gérard Philipe
45 Gina Lollobrigida
46 Michel Simon
47 Raimu
48 Fernandel
49 Michele Morgan
50 Charles Boyer
51 Anna Magnani
52 Maurice Chevalier
53 Alec Guinness
54 Jean Gabin
55 Louis Jouvet
56 Lionel Barrymore
57 John Gilbert
58 Laurence Olivier
59 Vivien Leigh
60 Clark Gable
61 Spencer Tracy
62 Myrna Loy
63 William Powell
64 Fred Astaire
65 Stepin Fetchit
66 Adolphe Menjou
67 Erich von Stroheim
68 Warner Oland
69 Lon Chaney
70 Charles Laughton
71 Edward G. Robinson
72 Peter Lorre
73 Boris Karloff
74 Bela Lugosi
75 Joan Crawford

Ferber, Edna 128–29
Ferrer, José 102
FIDDLER ON THE ROOF 26, 27
Fields, W. C. 24, 78
Finch, Peter 106
Fonda, Henry 19, 80
Fontanne, Lynn 128–29
FORTY CARATS 59
42nd STREET 76
FUNNY GIRL 50
FUNNY THING HAPPENED ON THE WAY TO THE FORUM, A 20

Gable, Clark 79, 95
Gallagher, Helen 54–55
Gardner, Ava 101
Garland, Judy 83, 136
Gelber, Jack 149
GEORGE M! 58
GOING IN STYLE 115
Goldwater, Barry 138
Gough, Michael 86–87
Graham, Martha 15
Grant, Cary 84
GRAPES OF WRATH, THE 80
Grey, Joel 58
Grodin, Charles 116
GUESS WHO'S COMING TO DINNER? 107
Guillaume, Ralph 52
Guinness, Alec 86–87, 103, 112–13
GUYS AND DOLLS 45

Haas, Dolly 4, 22–23, 31, 35
Hamilton, Richard 73
Hardy (Oliver), Laurel and 19, 119
Harris, Julie 59
Hawkins, Trish 74
Hawn, Goldie 109, 116
Hearn, George 75
Heckart, Eileen 109
HELLO, DOLLY! 21
Hepburn, Katharine 107
Hines, Gregory 66
Hirsch, Judd 74
Hirschfeld, Al 2, 7–10, 16, 37, 43, 77, 117, 153
Hirschfeld, Dolly see Haas, Dolly
Hirschfeld, Nina 4, 31–35
Holm, Celeste 47
Hope, Bob 19, 98
HORSE'S MOUTH, THE 86–87
Houghton, Katharine 107

I DO! I DO! 56
INHERIT THE WIND 92
INVITATION TO A MARCH 47
IRMA LA DOUCE 100
IT SEEMS LIKE OLD TIMES 116

Jackson, Anne 48
Jackson, Glenda 110
Johnson, Lyndon 138
Jones, Tom 151
Julia, Raul 68–69

159

Karloff, Boris 134
Kaufman, George S. 128–29
Kaye, Danny 135
Kaye, Stubby 45
Kelly, Gene 81, 92, 151
Kelly, Grace 82
Kerr, Deborah 101
Kitt, Eartha 61
Kopit, Arthur 149

Lanchester, Elsa 112–13
Langella, Frank 114
Lansbury, Angela 57
LAST ANGRY MAN, THE 90
Laughton, Charles 79
Laurel (Stan), and Hardy 19, 119
Leigh, Vivien 102
Lemmon, Jack 19, 88–89, 91, 100, 111
Lenya, Lotte 48
Levene, Sam 45
Lindfors, Viveca 48
Lithgow, John 65
LIVE FROM NEW YORK 64
Lunt, Alfred 128–29
Lyon, Sue 101

MacLaine, Shirley 91, 97, 100
MAME 57
MAN IN THE GLASS BOOTH, THE 58
March, Frederic 92
Marchand, Nancy 73
Martin, Mary 44, 56
Marsh, Jean 63
Marvin, Lee 102
Marx Brothers (Chico, Groucho, Harpo) 19, 118, 146
Marx, Groucho 24
Mason, Marsha 115
Matisse, Henri 155
Matthau, Walter 19, 54
McCABE AND MRS. MILLER 108
McNeil, Claudia 94
Mercouri, Melina 85
Merrill, Gary 73
Miller, Ann 70
Miller, Arthur 148
Miller, Jonathan 49
MIRACLE WORKER, THE 96–97
MISFITS, THE 95

Mitchum, Robert 97
Monroe, Marilyn 88–89, 95
Moore, Dudley 49
Moore, Garry 20, 22, 23
Moore, Melba 62
Morgan, Harry 92
Morgan, Mike 86–87
MORNING'S AT SEVEN 73
Mostel, Zero 9, 19, 20, 26, 27
Movies, The 122–23
Muni, Paul 90
MURDER BY DEATH 112–13
MUTINY ON THE BOUNTY 79

Natwick, Mildred 65
Nelligan, Kate 114
NEVER ON SUNDAY 85
New York Shakespeare Festival, The 68–69
NIGHT AND DAY 66
NIGHT OF THE IGUANA, THE 101
Nina, see Hirschfeld, Nina
1940'S RADIO HOUR, THE 70
Niven, David 112–13
NUTS 71

O'Casey, Sean 121
ODD COUPLE, THE 54
OLD MAN AND THE SEA, THE 88
Oliver, Thelma 54–55
Olivier, Laurence 114
ON THE WATERFRONT 82
Orbach, Jerry 76
O'Sullivan, Maureen 73
OTHELLO 68–69
OTHERWISE ENGAGED 60

Paar, Jack 125
Parker, Dorothy 128–29
"Peace in Our Time"—Neville Chamberlain 42
Pedi, Tom 45
Perelman, S. J. 143
Perkins, Anthony 67
PHOTO FINISH 51
Picasso, Pablo 154
Playwrights at Work 149
Pleasence, Donald 58
Poitier, Sidney 94, 107
PORGY AND BESS 52

Presley, Elvis 142
Preston, Robert 56, 139
Prince of Wales, The 12
PRISONER OF SECOND AVENUE, THE 111
Public bar 40
Pully, B. S. 45

Radner, Gilda 64
RAISIN IN THE SUN, A 94
Rathbone, Basil 44
Ricci, Marlene 151
Richardson, Jack 149
Richardson, Ralph 103
ROAD TO HONG KONG, THE 98
Robards, Jason, Jr. 19, 59
Robbins, Jerome 93
Rogers, Kenny 150
ROMANTIC COMEDY 67
Rooney, Pat, Sr. 45
Roosevelt, Franklin Delano 120
Rounds, David 73
ROYAL WEDDING 99
Ruehmann, Heinz 102
Russell, Bertrand 126

Saint, Eva Marie 82
Sands, Diana 59
SATURDAY NIGHT LIVE 64
Segal, George 104–5, 110
Sellers, Peter 112–13
Seltzer, Daniel 71
Serviette au Cou, La 41
Sharif, Omar 103
Sherwood, Robert 128–29
SHIP OF FOOLS 102
Signoret, Simone 102
Silver, Johnny 45
Sinatra, Frank 151
SINGIN' IN THE RAIN 81
Skelton, Red 131
Smith, Maggie 66, 112–13
SOME LIKE IT HOT 88–89
SOUTH PACIFIC 44
Soviet worker, Moscow 38
Stamp, Terence 106
STAR IS BORN, A 83
Strasberg, Lee 115
Streisand, Barbra 50
SUGAR BABIES 70

Sullivan, Ed 133
SUNSET BOULEVARD 80
Swanson, Gloria 80
SWEET CHARITY 54–55

TALLEY'S FOLLY 74
Taylor, Elizabeth 104–5
Thomas, Danny 133
Thomas, Terry 134
TIMBUKTU! 61, 62
TO CATCH A THIEF 84
TOUCH OF CLASS, A 110
Tracy, Spencer 88, 92, 107
TRANSFIGURATION OF BENNO BLIMPIE, THE 60
TWO FOR THE SEESAW 97
Twomey, Anne 71
TWO'S COMPANY 46
Tyler, Veronica 52

Ustinov, Peter 51

Verdon, Gwen, 19, 54–55
Von Stroheim, Erich 80
Voskovec, George 48

Wager, Michael 48
WAITING FOR GODOT 138
Walker, Nancy 112–13
Walsh, Kay 86–87
Warfield, William 52
WATCH ON THE RHINE 75
WE BOMBED IN NEW HAVEN 59
Werner, Oskar 102
Wertmuller, Lina 147
WEST SIDE STORY 93
WHO'S AFRAID OF VIRGINIA WOOLF? 104–5
WHOSE LIFE IS IT ANYWAY? 63
Wilder, Billy 100
Williams, Andy 151
Williams, Tennessee 148
Wilson, Elizabeth 73
Winwood, Estelle 112–13
Wise, Robert 93
Woollcott, Alexander 128–29
Wright, Teresa 73
Wynn, Ed 19, 124

York, Dick 92

ACKNOWLEDGEMENTS

The author wishes to thank the following for paying his room rent across many years and for permission to reproduce some of the drawings in this book: *The New York Times;* Columbia Broadcasting System; *Saturday Review;* National Broadcasting Company, Inc.; The Museum of Modern Art; Whitney Museum of American Art.

The editors gratefully acknowledge the assistance and cooperation of Stanley R. Goldmark of The Margo Feiden Galleries.